JUMBLE®
Ever After

A Lifetime of Puzzles!

**Henri Arnold,
Bob Lee,
Michael Argirion,
Jeff Knurek, &
David L. Hoyt**

TRIUMPH
BOOKS

Jumble® is a registered trademark
of Tribune Media Services, Inc.
Copyright © 2020 by Tribune Media Services, Inc.
All rights reserved.
This book is available in quantity at special discounts
for your group or organization.

For further information, contact:
Triumph Books LLC
814 North Franklin Street
Chicago, Illinois 60610
Phone: (312) 337-0747
www.triumphbooks.com

Printed in U.S.A.
ISBN: 978-1-62937-785-8

Design by Sue Knopf

Contents

JUMBLE®
Ever After

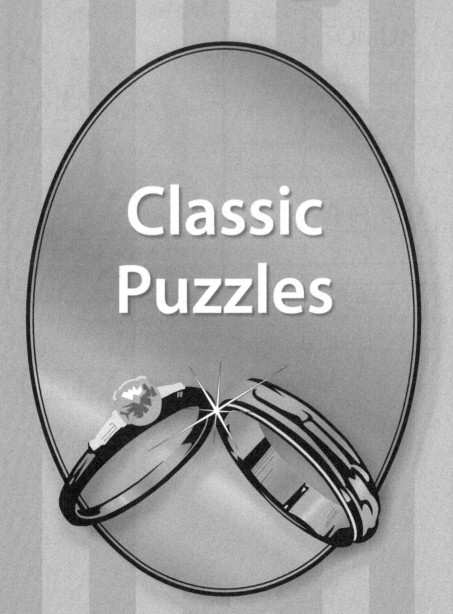

Classic Puzzles

JUMBLE®

Unscramble these four Jumbles, one letter
to each square, to form four ordinary words.

HUMOT

FREVE

SCEPHY

TILPUF

WHAT THE
TAXIDERMIST'S
PERSONALITY
CERTAINLY WAS.

Now arrange the circled letters
to form the surprise answer, as
suggested by the above cartoon.

Print answer here " ⬡⬡⬡⬡⬡⬡ "

JUMBLE®

Unscramble these four Jumbles, one letter
to each square, to form four ordinary words.

SOEBE

MABLY

REMMAH

HYROTE

Any place is better than here

PEOPLE WITH
WANDERLUST SELDOM
FEEL THIS.

Now arrange the circled letters
to form the surprise answer, as
suggested by the above cartoon.

**Print answer
here**   AT ☐☐☐☐☐ ☐☐ ☐☐☐☐☐

3

JUMBLE®

Unscramble these four Jumbles, one letter to each square, to form four ordinary words.

Turns my stomach

SEGUS

TAREF

DINKAP

BERBOR

THE LONGER THAT SERGEANT STAYED IN THE ARMY---

Now arrange the circled letters to form the surprise answer, as suggested by the above cartoon.

Print answer here THE " ⬡⬡⬡⬡⬡⬡ " HE ⬡⬡⬡

JUMBLE®

Unscramble these four Jumbles, one letter
to each square, to form four ordinary words.

ROLYG

ERNIL

BLABED

GOFTER

WHAT HER ATTEMPTS
AT COOKING
BROUGHT HIM.

Now arrange the circled letters
to form the surprise answer, as
suggested by the above cartoon.

Print answer here

JUMBLE®

Unscramble these four Jumbles, one letter
to each square, to form four ordinary words.

VELDE

CROAG

KEBTUC

NAMALY

WHAT WAS
MICHELANGELO'S
FAVORITE DESSERT?

Now arrange the circled letters
to form the surprise answer, as
suggested by the above cartoon.

Print answer here

JUMBLE.

Unscramble these four Jumbles, one letter
to each square, to form four ordinary words.

FOREY

NADAP

YULIBS

BELMAG

HOW THE SPONGE
DIVERS FOUND
THEIR WORK.

Now arrange the circled letters
to form the surprise answer, as
suggested by the above cartoon.

Print answer here " ⃝⃝⃝⃝⃝⃝⃝⃝⃝⃝ "

JUMBLE®

Unscramble these four Jumbles, one letter to each square, to form four ordinary words.

REPIK

TOABB

GAHOME

CRYGLE

Hey—I'm alive!!

WHAT LIGHTNING GAVE THE FRANKEN-STEIN MONSTER.

Now arrange the circled letters to form the surprise answer, as suggested by the above cartoon.

Print answer here A ☐☐☐ " ☐☐☐☐☐☐ "

JUMBLE®

Unscramble these four Jumbles, one letter
to each square, to form four ordinary words.

NYSOW

THACC

DILANI

TRYAGE

Here's a dime — go out
and mow my lawn

HOW THE MISER
GOT RICH.

Now arrange the circled letters
to form the surprise answer, as
suggested by the above cartoon.

Print answer here   THE " ⬡⬡⬡⬡⬡⬡ " ⬡⬡⬡

JUMBLE®

Unscramble these four Jumbles, one letter
to each square, to form four ordinary words.

NIHKT

INVEX

SMEFLY

FAISAR

These new
forms are
something
else

WHAT THE
FISHERMAN'S GROSS
INCOME WAS.

Now arrange the circled letters
to form the surprise answer, as
suggested by the above cartoon.

Print
answer
here

⬡⬡⬡⬡ AS ⬡⬡⬡ " ⬡⬡⬡ "

JUMBLE®

Unscramble these four Jumbles, one letter
to each square, to form four ordinary words.

LASIE

CHACO

GERROF

SUREDS

There'll be others who will
have the real power

WHAT THAT MATH
WHIZ WHO ROSE TO
THE TOP OF THE
FIRM ENDED UP AS.

Now arrange the circled letters
to form the surprise answer, as
suggested by the above cartoon.

*Print answer
here* THE

JUMBLE.

Unscramble these four Jumbles, one letter
to each square, to form four ordinary words.

DYNAH

MAUSE

WOELLY

SUDSIC

SLAP!

Hey!

WHAT THE HIGHWAY
MAINTENANCE MAN
WAS TOLD TO DO.

Now arrange the circled letters
to form the surprise answer, as
suggested by the above cartoon.

*Print
answer
here*

"   "

JUMBLE®

Unscramble these four Jumbles, one letter to each square, to form four ordinary words.

KAFLE

LOMOB

TRUFUE

ENGOUT

HOW TO SILENCE A "LOUD" TIE.

Now arrange the circled letters to form the surprise answer, as suggested by the above cartoon.

Print answer here ◯◯◯ A " ◯◯◯◯◯◯◯◯ "

JUMBLE®

Unscramble these four Jumbles, one letter to each square, to form four ordinary words.

RYRUH

NOIBS

STRAIG

DROFEK

A risky way to make a living, I'd say

WHAT THE PRO-
FESSIONAL CRAP-
SHOOTER'S BUSINESS
MUST HAVE BEEN.

Now arrange the circled letters to form the surprise answer, as suggested by the above cartoon.

Print answer here " ◯◯◯◯◯ "

JUMBLE®

Unscramble these four Jumbles, one letter
to each square, to form four ordinary words.

ALLEG

SOOME

YARFER

CHUPIC

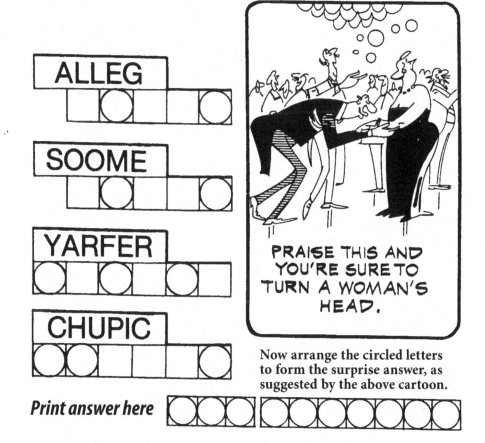

PRAISE THIS AND
YOU'RE SURE TO
TURN A WOMAN'S
HEAD.

Now arrange the circled letters
to form the surprise answer, as
suggested by the above cartoon.

Print answer here

JUMBLE®

Unscramble these four Jumbles, one letter to each square, to form four ordinary words.

ONLOY

UNFOT

NAPHOR

RAGUTI

Ho hum

WHY THEY FOUND THE NUDIST CAMP SO BORING.

Now arrange the circled letters to form the surprise answer, as suggested by the above cartoon.

Print answer here ⬡⬡⬡⬡⬡⬡⬡ WENT ⬡⬡

JUMBLE®

Unscramble these four Jumbles, one letter
to each square, to form four ordinary words.

DORAH

SULLK

UNPOWT

RIDOLF

HOW THE MANICURIST
REJECTED HIS
PROPOSAL OF
MARRIAGE.

Now arrange the circled letters
to form the surprise answer, as
suggested by the above cartoon.

Print answer here ◯◯◯ ◯◯ ◯◯◯◯◯

JUMBLE®

Unscramble these four Jumbles, one letter
to each square, to form four ordinary words.

LINAF

DRYBE

UNNACE

RUHLOY

I couldn't agree
with you more

ANOTHER NAME
FOR A DIALOGUE.

Now arrange the circled letters
to form the surprise answer, as
suggested by the above cartoon.

*Print
answer
here*   A ⬡⬡⬡⬡⬡⬡⬡ " ⬡⬡⬡⬡ "

JUMBLE®

Unscramble these four Jumbles, one letter
to each square, to form four ordinary words.

GANTE

HEGIT

TRYGEN

DRIMBO

SHE WAS ALWAYS
SURE TO KEEP
A SECRET---

Now arrange the circled letters
to form the surprise answer, as
suggested by the above cartoon.

Print answer here

JUMBLE®

Unscramble these four Jumbles, one letter
to each square, to form four ordinary words.

DAHEA

BICAN

SCOFIA

PIMNED

APPARENTLY IT'S
A SIGN OF GOOD
MANNERS TO PUT
UP WITH THIS.

Now arrange the circled letters
to form the surprise answer, as
suggested by the above cartoon.

Print answer here ⟨○○○⟩ ⟨○○○○⟩

JUMBLE®

Unscramble these four Jumbles, one letter
to each square, to form four ordinary words.

DUMIO

WOPHO

CAGNEY

PRAMCE

WHAT THE FIRST
DAY OF THE
WEEK CAN BE.

Now arrange the circled letters
to form the surprise answer, as
suggested by the above cartoon.

Print answer here " ◯◯◯◯◯ " ◯◯◯

JUMBLE®

Unscramble these four Jumbles, one letter
to each square, to form four ordinary words.

SOGOE

KLEAN

TYPAIR

GEAVAS

WHAT THEIR
BABIES' BEDROOM
WAS CALLED.

Now arrange the circled letters
to form the surprise answer, as
suggested by the above cartoon.

Print answer here THE " ◯◯◯◯◯◯◯ "

JUMBLE®

Unscramble these four Jumbles, one letter
to each square, to form four ordinary words.

GLONI

UGOBS

FROGLE

GROAND

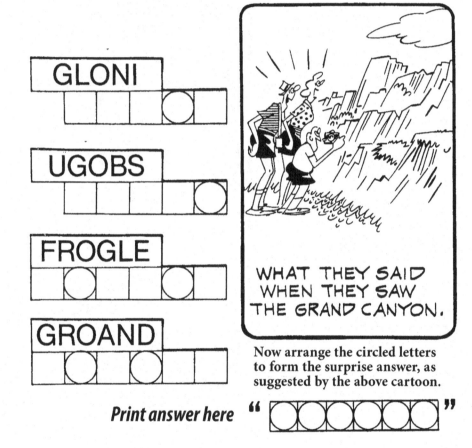

WHAT THEY SAID
WHEN THEY SAW
THE GRAND CANYON.

Now arrange the circled letters
to form the surprise answer, as
suggested by the above cartoon.

Print answer here " ⬡⬡⬡⬡⬡⬡ "

JUMBLE®

Unscramble these four Jumbles, one letter
to each square, to form four ordinary words.

TYSUL

YOANG

SPYGUM

PERRAY

KEEPING UP WITH
THE JONESES
MIGHT ALSO IN-
VOLVE KEEPING
UP WITH THESE.

Now arrange the circled letters
to form the surprise answer, as
suggested by the above cartoon.

Print answer here THE ⬡⬡⬡⬡⬡⬡⬡⬡⬡

JUMBLE®

Unscramble these four Jumbles, one letter
to each square, to form four ordinary words.

KOBOR

GOMOR

NAUSED

RICHEP

Ugh!

WHAT THOSE
SOCIETY "CRUMBS"
WERE HELD
TOGETHER BY.

Now arrange the circled letters
to form the surprise answer, as
suggested by the above cartoon.

Print answer here " ⬡⬡⬡⬡⬡ "

JUMBLE®

Unscramble these four Jumbles, one letter
to each square, to form four ordinary words.

NISHY

JECET

REBURB

MAIDDY

Too bad he wasn't
a nicer person

WHAT THE
BILLIONAIRE
LEFT WHEN HE
DIED.

Now arrange the circled letters
to form the surprise answer, as
suggested by the above cartoon.

Print answer here ◯◯◯◯ TO BE ◯◯◯◯◯◯◯◯

JUMBLE®
Ever After

Daily
Puzzles

JUMBLE®

Unscramble these four Jumbles, one letter to each square, to form four ordinary words.

YOIRN

TIMAD

MOFTEN

BOULED

Our little dolls

PERMISSIVE PARENTS DON'T MIND WHEN THEIR KIDS THIS.

Now arrange the circled letters to form the surprise answer, as suggested by the above cartoon.

Print answer here ⬡⬡⬡ ' ⬡ ⬡⬡⬡⬡

JUMBLE®

Unscramble these four Jumbles, one letter
to each square, to form four ordinary words.

ACCOO

DUTOO

TREBUT

ENTHIZ

You've had enough!

HE DOESN'T LIKE
TO BE ORDERED
AROUND UNLESS
IT'S THIS.

Now arrange the circled letters
to form the surprise answer, as
suggested by the above cartoon.

**Print answer
here**   A ☐☐☐☐☐☐ OF ☐☐☐☐☐

JUMBLE®

Unscramble these four Jumbles, one letter
to each square, to form four ordinary words.

GORRI

AMGUT

LOCASE

INTOAR

WHAT SHE WISHED
HER ADMIRERS
WOULD PRACTICE.

Now arrange the circled letters
to form the surprise answer, as
suggested by the above cartoon.

Print answer
here   "   "

JUMBLE®

Unscramble these four Jumbles, one letter
to each square, to form four ordinary words.

RIGMY

TRUPE

DELAUF

STERJE

Those were the good old days when I controlled all that money

You'll have some special privileges here

WHAT AN UNETHICAL TRUSTEE SOMETIMES ENDS UP AS.

Now arrange the circled letters
to form the surprise answer, as
suggested by the above cartoon.

Print answer here

JUMBLE®

Unscramble these four Jumbles, one letter
to each square, to form four ordinary words.

LUFAW

RAPPE

STAJEM

HERNID

I don't know what he's got to be snooty about

WHAT NEPOTISM MEANS IN THE FIELD OF EMPLOYMENT.

Now arrange the circled letters
to form the surprise answer, as
suggested by the above cartoon.

Print answer here TO ☐☐☐ ON "☐☐☐☐☐"

JUMBLE®

Unscramble these four Jumbles, one letter
to each square, to form four ordinary words.

RYKUM

HIEWL

CLAJAK

DORRAM

A FOUR-LETTER
WORD THAT SOME
PEOPLE FIND MOST
"OBJECTIONABLE."

Now arrange the circled letters
to form the surprise answer, as
suggested by the above cartoon.

Print answer here " ◯◯◯◯ "

JUMBLE®

Unscramble these four Jumbles, one letter
to each square, to form four ordinary words.

LOBOD

AXTEC

TRIMAN

GARUJA

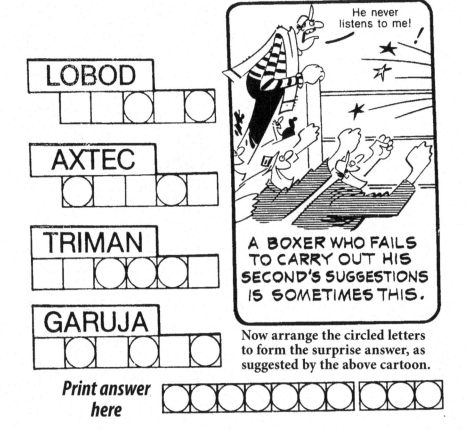

He never
listens to me!

A BOXER WHO FAILS
TO CARRY OUT HIS
SECOND'S SUGGESTIONS
IS SOMETIMES THIS.

Now arrange the circled letters
to form the surprise answer, as
suggested by the above cartoon.

**Print answer
here**

JUMBLE®

Unscramble these four Jumbles, one letter to each square, to form four ordinary words.

YIXTS

BABIR

SAILEY

LEARNY

ONE IS NOT AT LIBERTY TO TAKE THIS WITH OTHERS.

Now arrange the circled letters to form the surprise answer, as suggested by the above cartoon.

Print answer here

JUMBLE®

Unscramble these four Jumbles, one letter
to each square, to form four ordinary words.

SYNIO

BLEER

ADUMAR

QULLAS

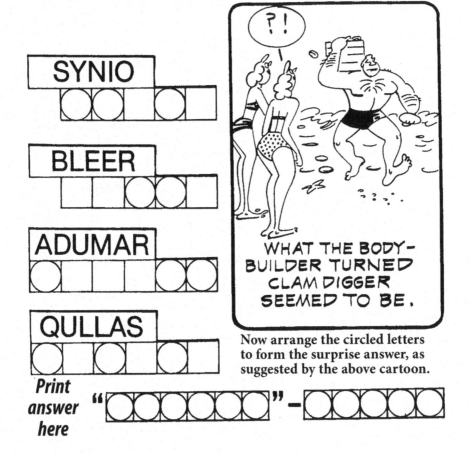

?!

WHAT THE BODY-
BUILDER TURNED
CLAM DIGGER
SEEMED TO BE.

Now arrange the circled letters
to form the surprise answer, as
suggested by the above cartoon.

Print
answer
here

"⬡⬡⬡⬡⬡⬡" – ⬡⬡⬡⬡⬡

JUMBLE®

Unscramble these four Jumbles, one letter to each square, to form four ordinary words.

FYNAC

TENFO

LENZOZ

ARIDAL

WHAT THAT TIRESOME SPEECHMAKER COULD NOT BE AFTER HE WAS CALLED ON.

Now arrange the circled letters to form the surprise answer, as suggested by the above cartoon.

Print answer here

JUMBLE®

Unscramble these four Jumbles, one letter
to each square, to form four ordinary words.

HYDUC

SURUP

TOBENN

IMUSSE

Wouldn't hurt if you both
lost a few pounds

HIS WORST FAULT
IS TELLING OTHER
PEOPLE ---

Now arrange the circled letters
to form the surprise answer, as
suggested by the above cartoon.

Print answer here

JUMBLE®

Unscramble these four Jumbles, one letter to each square, to form four ordinary words.

LAIGE

ARVEG

CHABRE

NENFLE

MATERNITY

Wow! I'm a dad!

WHAT A BRAND-NEW FATHER IS ABOUT TO ENTER INTO.

Now arrange the circled letters to form the surprise answer, as suggested by the above cartoon.

Print answer here

A ◯◯◯◯◯◯◯◯◯ WORLD

JUMBLE®

Unscramble these four Jumbles, one letter
to each square, to form four ordinary words.

That's the place
where his highness
kissed my hand

Next you'll
see me dance
with the
princess

WHAT MANY PEOPLE
START OUT ON,
RIGHT AFTER THEY
RETURN HOME
FROM A VACATION.

PAUNC

ARCTT

GIRDIF

DOINIE

Now arrange the circled letters
to form the surprise answer, as
suggested by the above cartoon.

Print answer here AN ⬡⬡⬡ ⬡⬡⬡⬡⬡

JUMBLE®

Unscramble these four Jumbles, one letter
to each square, to form four ordinary words.

ANGLD

TIDEF

BELMIN

SWORDY

WHAT A PERSON
WHO'S ALWAYS
KICKING SELDOM HAS.

Now arrange the circled letters
to form the surprise answer, as
suggested by the above cartoon.

*Print
answer
here*

A ◯◯◯ TO ◯◯◯◯◯◯ ◯◯

JUMBLE®

Unscramble these four Jumbles, one letter
to each square, to form four ordinary words.

LOGUM

PUJEL

GREDIB

ONCOMM

Look at that idiot

IF A PEDESTRIAN
IS PRONE TO BE
CARELESS HE MIGHT
END UP THIS WAY.

Now arrange the circled letters
to form the surprise answer, as
suggested by the above cartoon.

Print answer here ◯◯◯◯◯

JUMBLE®

Unscramble these four Jumbles, one letter
to each square, to form four ordinary words.

INFIS

LASIA

TANNIF

YERSIM

I took it off the
shelf, dear

WHAT MANY AN
AMATEUR GARDENER
GETS FOR HIS PAINS.

Now arrange the circled letters
to form the surprise answer, as
suggested by the above cartoon.

Print answer here

JUMBLE.

Unscramble these four Jumbles, one letter
to each square, to form four ordinary words.

GYNAM

CAUMS

DYLOUB

THARGE

My rich uncle isn't
long for this world

A MAN WHO IS
ALWAYS ASKING FOR
A LOAN IS APT TO
BE LEFT THIS.

Now arrange the circled letters
to form the surprise answer, as
suggested by the above cartoon.

Print answer here

JUMBLE®

Unscramble these four Jumbles, one letter
to each square, to form four ordinary words.

LONEV

DAMAR

GOBNEY

MESECH

CREDIT MIGHT BE
THE MEANS TO
LIVE LIKE THIS.

Now arrange the circled letters
to form the surprise answer, as
suggested by the above cartoon.

**Print
answer
here** ◯◯◯◯◯◯◯ ONE'S ◯◯◯◯◯

JUMBLE®

Unscramble these four Jumbles, one letter to each square, to form four ordinary words.

FREGI

SAUPE

TORICE

MUNCOL

No ticket, no coat

YOU CAN'T GET RID OF A BAD TEMPER BY DOING THIS.

Now arrange the circled letters to form the surprise answer, as suggested by the above cartoon.

Print answer here

JUMBLE®

Unscramble these four Jumbles, one letter
to each square, to form four ordinary words.

USHOE

WARLC

TOCCUL

HINCUR

ANOTHER NAME
FOR THE TIME YOU
SPEND GOING HOME
FROM WORK.

Now arrange the circled letters
to form the surprise answer, as
suggested by the above cartoon.

*Print answer
here* THE " ☐☐☐☐☐ " ☐☐☐☐

JUMBLE.

Unscramble these four Jumbles, one letter
to each square, to form four ordinary words.

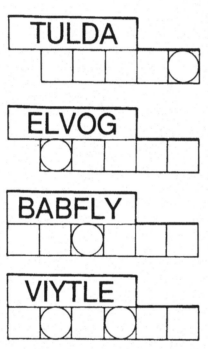

TULDA

ELVOG

BABFLY

VIYTLE

I'd like to read the
prospectus first. I'll
get back to you

ADD THIS ON FOR
YOUR PROTECTION,
IF YOU'RE ABOUT
TO INVEST.

Now arrange the circled letters
to form the surprise answer, as
suggested by the above cartoon.

Print answer here " — ⬡⬡⬡⬡⬡ "

JUMBLE®

Unscramble these four Jumbles, one letter to each square, to form four ordinary words.

SOSBA

YERAW

LAUTRI

COSMAT

I can guess what he's been up to

HIS CLOTHES TELL YOU A LOT ABOUT THIS.

Now arrange the circled letters to form the surprise answer, as suggested by the above cartoon.

Print answer here HIS "⬡⬡⬡⬡⬡" – ⬡⬡⬡⬡⬡⬡

JUMBLE®

Unscramble these four Jumbles, one letter to each square, to form four ordinary words.

STYRT

CAULD

LIRBED

GARNAH

HE'S OLD ENOUGH TO KNOW BETTER, BUT TOO OLD TO DO THIS.

Now arrange the circled letters to form the surprise answer, as suggested by the above cartoon.

Print answer here

JUMBLE®

Unscramble these four Jumbles, one letter to each square, to form four ordinary words.

TELLU

GUFED

SIPVLE

PRUBES

WHAT A GOOD INSECTICIDE MIGHT BE.

Now arrange the circled letters to form the surprise answer, as suggested by the above cartoon.

Print answer here   A "⬡⬡⬡⬡" ⬡⬡⬡⬡⬡⬡⬡

JUMBLE®

Unscramble these four Jumbles, one letter to each square, to form four ordinary words.

GOGSY

CRANF

MECION

COMIAT

IT'S HARD TO RAISE A CHILD, ESPECIALLY WHEN IT'S THIS.

Now arrange the circled letters to form the surprise answer, as suggested by the above cartoon.

Print answer here

JUMBLE®

Unscramble these four Jumbles, one letter to each square, to form four ordinary words.

SLYTE

CEENF

SIRNAP

STTURY

Here you go. I hope you enjoy camping.

Gee. Thanks!

Let's go set it up now.

THE CAMPERS ARE RECEIVING THEIR GIFTS RIGHT NOW . . . THEY ARE GETTING ----

Now arrange the circled letters to form the surprise answer, as suggested by the above cartoon.

Print answer here

"

JUMBLE®

Unscramble these four Jumbles, one letter to each square, to form four ordinary words.

PLEEO

FUYIN

STUMCO

ADFAIR

MEGLA MALL COMING SOON

How are we going to move all these?

Just start digging, I guess.

AFTER LOSING HIS LEASE, THE OWNER OF THE PLANT NURSERY WOULD BE ---

Now arrange the circled letters to form the surprise answer, as suggested by the above cartoon.

Print answer here

JUMBLE®

Unscramble these four Jumbles, one letter to each square, to form four ordinary words.

YDOLD

CHUMN

FAUNIR

LOHWOL

There's no room to build.

Let's move back to Earth.

CITIES MIGHT ONE DAY BE BUILT ON THE LUNAR SURFACE, WHICH COULD RESULT IN A ---

Now arrange the circled letters to form the surprise answer, as suggested by the above cartoon.

Print answer here

JUMBLE®

Unscramble these four Jumbles, one letter
to each square, to form four ordinary words.

AVIEW

SLIPO

UNEVEA

SWRAPL

Now, I need you to get fired
up and go throw some
touchdowns.

Nothing
gets to
him.

Cool as a
cucumber.

THE NEW QUARTERBACK
DIDN'T GET EXCITED ABOUT
MUCH. THE COACH WORRIED
THAT HE WAS TOO ———

Now arrange the circled letters
to form the surprise answer, as
suggested by the above cartoon.

Print answer here

JUMBLE.

Unscramble these four Jumbles, one letter
to each square, to form four ordinary words.

TMAID

SAYET

TELUTO

GEMNAT

If I could get the
capital to plant the
first section, I'd be
in business.

I'll get
your loan
started.

PLOT A

HONEYCRISPS

HE WANTED TO START
AN APPLE ORCHARD,
BUT TO GET IT GOING,
HE NEEDED ----

Now arrange the circled letters
to form the surprise answer, as
suggested by the above cartoon.

**Print answer
here**

JUMBLE®

Unscramble these four Jumbles, one letter
to each square, to form four ordinary words.

CAWYK

PRUNS

TALLEY

MEGEER

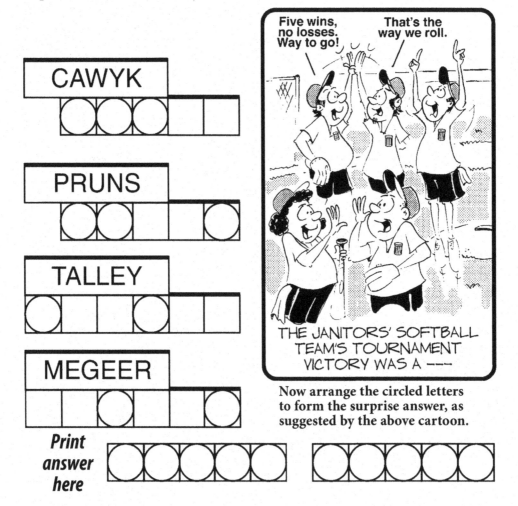

Five wins,
no losses.
Way to go!

That's the
way we roll.

THE JANITORS' SOFTBALL
TEAM'S TOURNAMENT
VICTORY WAS A ---

Now arrange the circled letters
to form the surprise answer, as
suggested by the above cartoon.

Print
answer
here

JUMBLE®

Unscramble these four Jumbles, one letter
to each square, to form four ordinary words.

GALVE

DRING

MAILSD

REARYT

I can't work
under these
conditions.

These –
students
deserve
better.

CONDITIONS AT THE
SCHOOL WERE ---

Now arrange the circled letters
to form the surprise answer, as
suggested by the above cartoon.

*Print answer
here*

JUMBLE®

Unscramble these four Jumbles, one letter
to each square, to form four ordinary words.

ROLYG

TYEHF

SUNFIE

REVONG

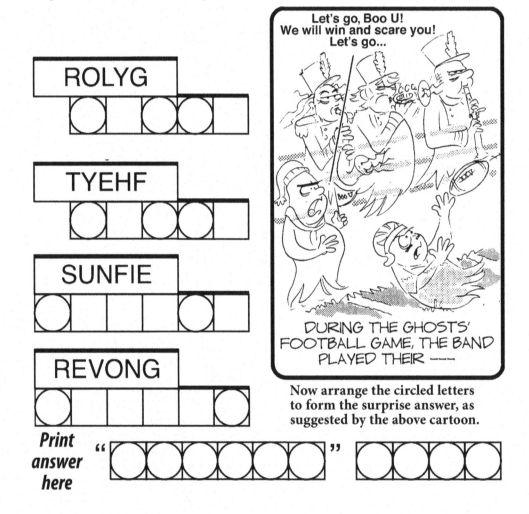

Let's go, Boo U!
We will win and scare you!
Let's go...

DURING THE GHOSTS'
FOOTBALL GAME, THE BAND
PLAYED THEIR ----

Now arrange the circled letters
to form the surprise answer, as
suggested by the above cartoon.

*Print
answer
here*   " ◯◯◯◯◯◯ "   ◯◯◯◯

JUMBLE®

Unscramble these four Jumbles, one letter to each square, to form four ordinary words.

SNIHY

OGGIN

SOWIMD

TANNIF

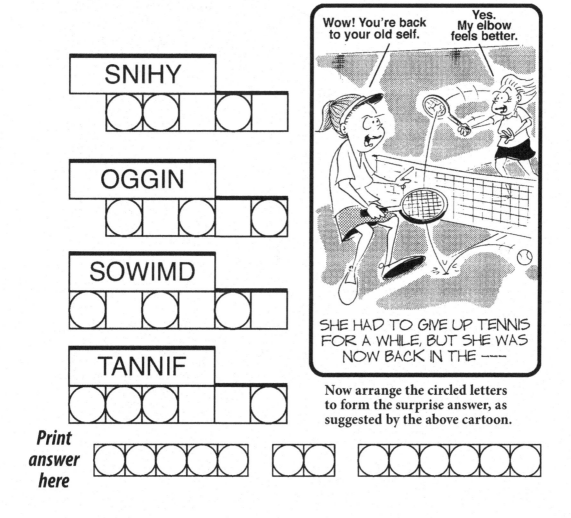

Wow! You're back to your old self.

Yes. My elbow feels better.

SHE HAD TO GIVE UP TENNIS FOR A WHILE, BUT SHE WAS NOW BACK IN THE ----

Now arrange the circled letters to form the surprise answer, as suggested by the above cartoon.

Print answer here

JUMBLE.

Unscramble these four Jumbles, one letter
to each square, to form four ordinary words.

DUGRO

FARET

RENROY

CUBENO

I can't believe
you're leaving. It
seems like you
just arrived.

My work here
is done.

THE CARPENTER WAS DONE
WITH THE NEW DOOR. HE
EXITED AFTER MAKING A ----

Now arrange the circled letters
to form the surprise answer, as
suggested by the above cartoon.

*Print
answer
here*

JUMBLE®

Unscramble these four Jumbles, one letter to each square, to form four ordinary words.

DOVIA

SHACO

LANFIE

HBRUCE

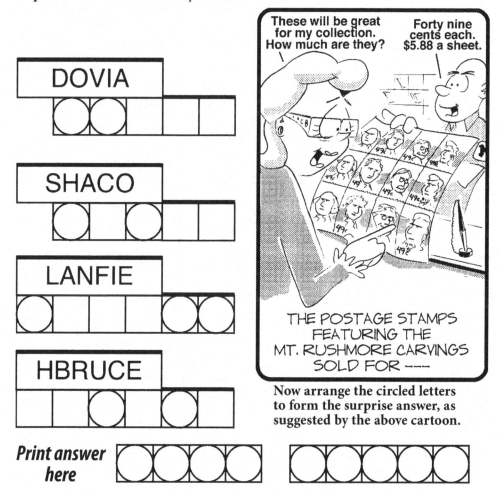

These will be great for my collection. How much are they?

Forty nine cents each. $5.88 a sheet.

THE POSTAGE STAMPS FEATURING THE MT. RUSHMORE CARVINGS SOLD FOR ----

Now arrange the circled letters to form the surprise answer, as suggested by the above cartoon.

Print answer here

JUMBLE®

Unscramble these four Jumbles, one letter to each square, to form four ordinary words.

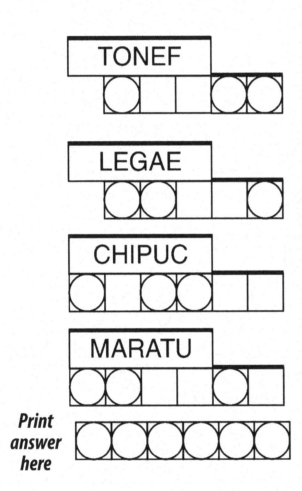

TONEF

LEGAE

CHIPUC

MARATU

Can I switch it over to the game?

I don't think so. My show is on.

HE WANTED TO CHANGE THE CHANNEL, BUT HE DIDN'T HAVE A ----

Now arrange the circled letters to form the surprise answer, as suggested by the above cartoon.

Print answer here

JUMBLE®

Unscramble these four Jumbles, one letter to each square, to form four ordinary words.

TAWEH

VEKOE

TERRGE

TONYOC

Let's go spend some of my winnings.

What else do you need?

HAPPY RETURNS

THE MORE TOURNAMENTS THE TENNIS PLAYER WON, THE MORE HE WAS ABLE TO ENJOY HIS ----

Now arrange the circled letters to form the surprise answer, as suggested by the above cartoon.

Print answer here

JUMBLE.

Unscramble these four Jumbles, one letter
to each square, to form four ordinary words.

SUHEO

NEPDU

PIHIMS

CIRBEK

It takes a brave man to hide
behind a curtain and
threaten a little girl. How do
you sleep at night?

EVEN THOUGH THE
SCARECROW DIDN'T HAVE A
BRAIN, HE ----

Now arrange the circled letters
to form the surprise answer, as
suggested by the above cartoon.

Print
answer
here

JUMBLE®

Unscramble these four Jumbles, one letter to each square, to form four ordinary words.

SUBOG

ALUTF

CEEPIA

GANCEL

HE STOLE SECOND AND NOW LED THE LEAGUE IN STEALS WHICH PLEASED HIS ----

Now arrange the circled letters to form the surprise answer, as suggested by the above cartoon.

Print answer here

JUMBLE®

Unscramble these four Jumbles, one letter
to each square, to form four ordinary words.

BRITO

VOSEH

TUPEYD

MOSTAC

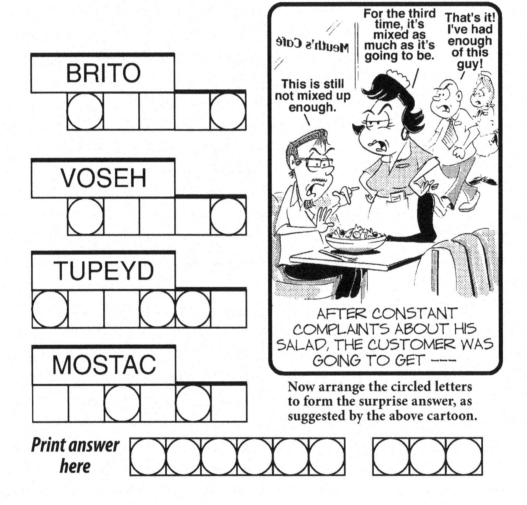

Məuği's Café

For the third
time, it's
mixed as
much as it's
going to be.

That's it!
I've had
enough
of this
guy!

This is still
not mixed up
enough.

AFTER CONSTANT
COMPLAINTS ABOUT HIS
SALAD, THE CUSTOMER WAS
GOING TO GET ----

Now arrange the circled letters
to form the surprise answer, as
suggested by the above cartoon.

**Print answer
here**
⬡⬡⬡⬡⬡⬡ ⬡⬡⬡

JUMBLE.

Unscramble these four Jumbles, one letter
to each square, to form four ordinary words.

BYRED

TEECL

TARLOM

RANBET

It's simple physics. The spit wad's
trajectory points at only one
person. It was you, James!

Brilliant,
Holmes!

WHEN SHERLOCK HOLMES
WAS IN GRAMMAR SCHOOL,
SOLVING A MYSTERY
WAS ---

Now arrange the circled letters
to form the surprise answer, as
suggested by the above cartoon.

*Print
answer
here*

JUMBLE®

Unscramble these four Jumbles, one letter
to each square, to form four ordinary words.

OINAP

KNOTE

EPLOPE

GURFAL

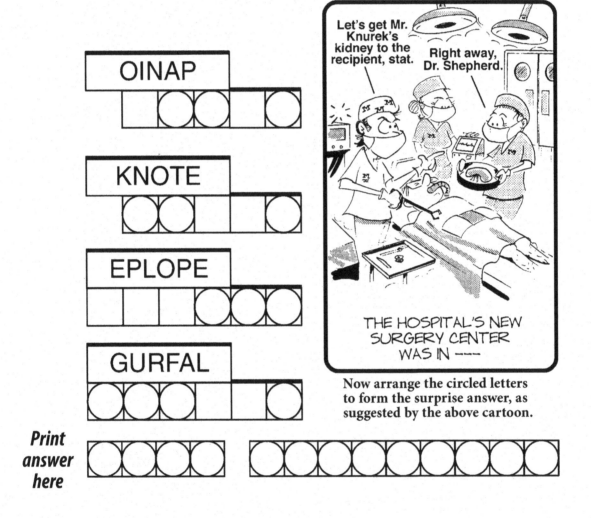

Let's get Mr.
Knurek's
kidney to the
recipient, stat.

Right away,
Dr. Shepherd.

THE HOSPITAL'S NEW
SURGERY CENTER
WAS IN ----

Now arrange the circled letters
to form the surprise answer, as
suggested by the above cartoon.

**Print
answer
here**

JUMBLE®

Unscramble these four Jumbles, one letter to each square, to form four ordinary words.

WLOVE

MEEEC

FISYTH

LARDLO

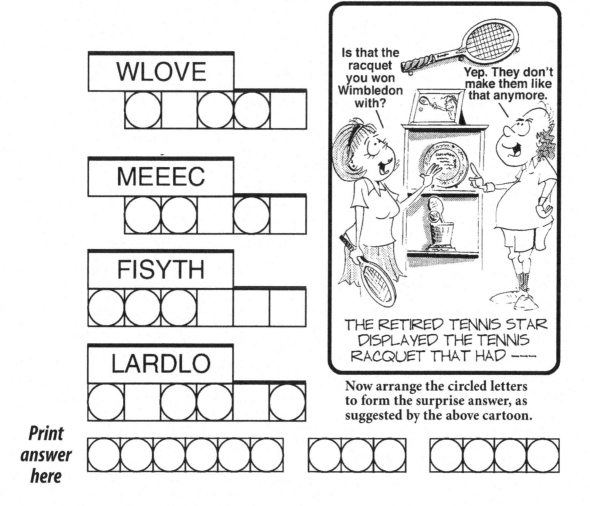

Is that the racquet you won Wimbledon with?

Yep. They don't make them like that anymore.

THE RETIRED TENNIS STAR DISPLAYED THE TENNIS RACQUET THAT HAD ---

Now arrange the circled letters to form the surprise answer, as suggested by the above cartoon.

Print answer here

JUMBLE.

Unscramble these four Jumbles, one letter to each square, to form four ordinary words.

LIDYO

AADRW

VALIJO

EATOGE

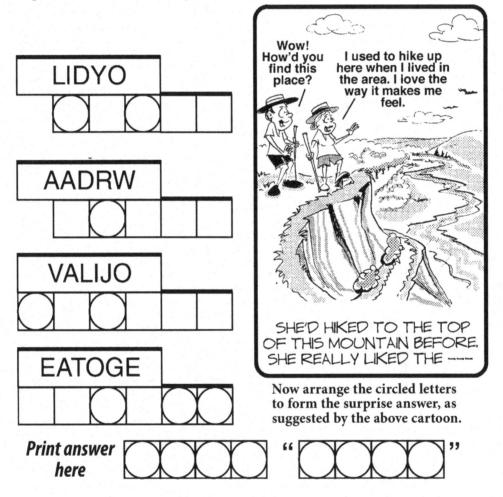

Wow! How'd you find this place?

I used to hike up here when I lived in the area. I love the way it makes me feel.

SHE'D HIKED TO THE TOP OF THIS MOUNTAIN BEFORE. SHE REALLY LIKED THE ----

Now arrange the circled letters to form the surprise answer, as suggested by the above cartoon.

Print answer here ⟨○○○○⟩ " ⟨○○○○⟩ "

JUMBLE®

Unscramble these four Jumbles, one letter
to each square, to form four ordinary words.

RIPRO

ESUGS

LAFBLE

NTIKET

Nothing gets past
him. We need to
extend his contract
right away.

I'll get our
lawyers
right on it!

THE SOCCER TEAM'S
GOALIE WAS AMAZING.
HE WAS A ----

Now arrange the circled letters
to form the surprise answer, as
suggested by the above cartoon.

Print answer here

JUMBLE.

Unscramble these four Jumbles, one letter
to each square, to form four ordinary words.

NUTSG

KRINB

SINCEK

TOCIXE

THE FIGHT BETWEEN
THE ELEPHANTS
FEATURED ----

Now arrange the circled letters
to form the surprise answer, as
suggested by the above cartoon.

*Print
answer
here*

JUMBLE®

Unscramble these four Jumbles, one letter
to each square, to form four ordinary words.

KLEAN

GRUDA

VERHIT

LAWPOL

TWISTED SISTER'S GIFTS

I'm almost
finished with the
Father's Day
cards.

Pick one
out for
Dad.

WHEN THE SISTERS
STARTED A BUSINESS
TOGETHER, THEY WERE ----

Now arrange the circled letters
to form the surprise answer, as
suggested by the above cartoon.

**Print
answer
here**

◯◯◯◯ - ◯◯◯◯◯◯◯

JUMBLE®

Unscramble these four Jumbles, one letter
to each square, to form four ordinary words.

USMAE

CLEET

VINDIE

FROFET

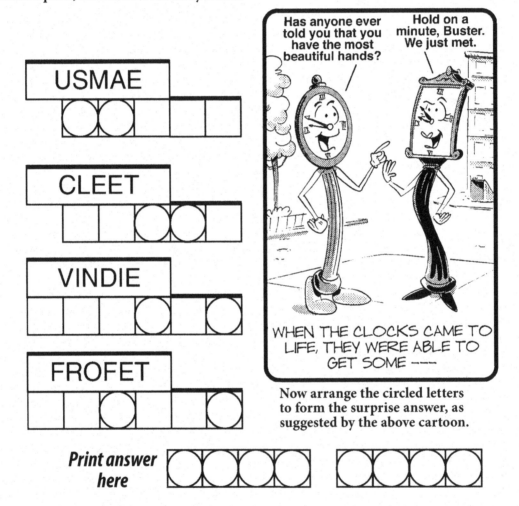

Has anyone ever told you that you have the most beautiful hands?

Hold on a minute, Buster. We just met.

WHEN THE CLOCKS CAME TO LIFE, THEY WERE ABLE TO GET SOME ----

Now arrange the circled letters
to form the surprise answer, as
suggested by the above cartoon.

Print answer here

JUMBLE®

Unscramble these four Jumbles, one letter to each square, to form four ordinary words.

FOCFS

NOONI

LEMTUL

HIGEYT

OK, Fifi. Now let's see who can find the most grubs.

I love that game.

THE DOGS THOUGHT THAT DIGGING UP THE YARD WAS A ----

Now arrange the circled letters to form the surprise answer, as suggested by the above cartoon.

Print answer here

"⬡⬡⬡⬡" ⬡⬡⬡ ⬡⬡ ⬡⬡⬡

JUMBLE®

Unscramble these four Jumbles, one letter
to each square, to form four ordinary words.

POMOH

THURT

SUSMIE

LINFEA

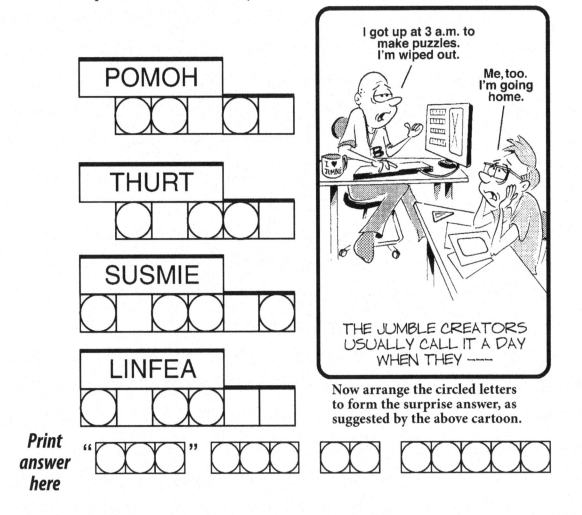

I got up at 3 a.m. to
make puzzles.
I'm wiped out.

Me, too.
I'm going
home.

THE JUMBLE CREATORS
USUALLY CALL IT A DAY
WHEN THEY ----

Now arrange the circled letters
to form the surprise answer, as
suggested by the above cartoon.

Print
answer
here

" ☐☐☐ " ☐☐☐☐ ☐☐ ☐☐☐☐☐☐

JUMBLE®

Unscramble these four Jumbles, one letter
to each square, to form four ordinary words.

WREAA

USHOE

SIFMIT

SEMTOD

Mmmmm.

Yum.

THE MOST COMMONLY
SPOKEN LANGUAGE IN THE
BAKERY WAS ----

Now arrange the circled letters
to form the surprise answer, as
suggested by the above cartoon.

Print answer "
here

JUMBLE.

Unscramble these four Jumbles, one letter
to each square, to form four ordinary words.

ROPIR

FINSF

RIMADE

NERDEG

Take that! All tied up now.

WHEN THE ZOMBIE TWINS
PLAYED HORSESHOES,
THEY WERE ----

Now arrange the circled letters
to form the surprise answer, as
suggested by the above cartoon.

Print
answer
here

JUMBLE®

Unscramble these four Jumbles, one letter
to each square, to form four ordinary words.

TUBAO

CANTE

LERONL

VINMER

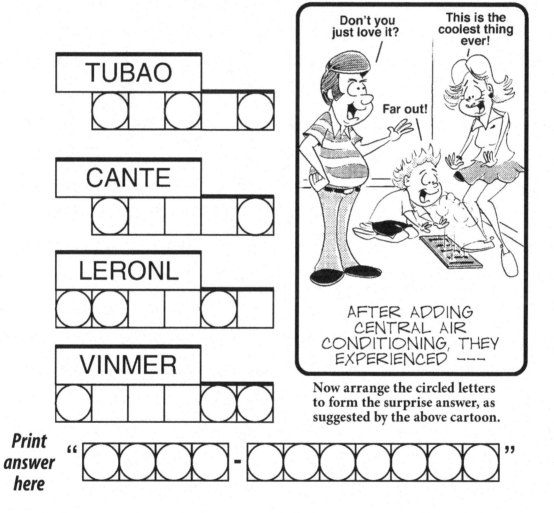

Don't you
just love it?

This is the
coolest thing
ever!

Far out!

AFTER ADDING
CENTRAL AIR
CONDITIONING, THEY
EXPERIENCED ---

Now arrange the circled letters
to form the surprise answer, as
suggested by the above cartoon.

**Print
answer
here**

"⬡⬡⬡⬡ - ⬡⬡⬡⬡⬡⬡⬡"

JUMBLE®

Unscramble these four Jumbles, one letter
to each square, to form four ordinary words.

SASTH

CCINY

RRIMPE

TENHIZ

We are
going to be
Americans!

ELLIS ISLAND WAS THE
GATEWAY FOR MILLIONS OF
IMMIGRANTS WHO ARRIVED
ON ----

Now arrange the circled letters
to form the surprise answer, as
suggested by the above cartoon.

*Print
answer
here*

JUMBLE®

Unscramble these four Jumbles, one letter to each square, to form four ordinary words.

CLEOL

NERUP

CASMTO

DINPTU

Wow! You look different at the vitamin store.

I'm on my way to my full-time job.

VITE MEN

THE MONEY SHE EARNED SELLING VITAMINS AND OTHER NUTRIENTS WAS ———

Now arrange the circled letters to form the surprise answer, as suggested by the above cartoon.

Print answer here

JUMBLE®

Unscramble these four Jumbles, one letter to each square, to form four ordinary words.

UDMHI

VARAL

FALBEF

TOLINO

It's so crowded, nobody comes anymore.

Really? You're quoting Yogi Berra?

THE CROWDED CHURCH SERVICE WAS ---

Now arrange the circled letters to form the surprise answer, as suggested by the above cartoon.

Print answer here

" ◯◯◯◯◯ - ◯◯◯◯ "

JUMBLE®

Unscramble these four Jumbles, one letter
to each square, to form four ordinary words.

ROIRP

EWLIH

VERGLA

CONHOP

ELECTRICITY IN
HEAVEN IS PROVIDED
BY A ---

Now arrange the circled letters
to form the surprise answer, as
suggested by the above cartoon.

Print
answer
here

JUMBLE®

Unscramble these four Jumbles, one letter
to each square, to form four ordinary words.

MPRAC

CYDIE

DUNNIW

NEDLEG

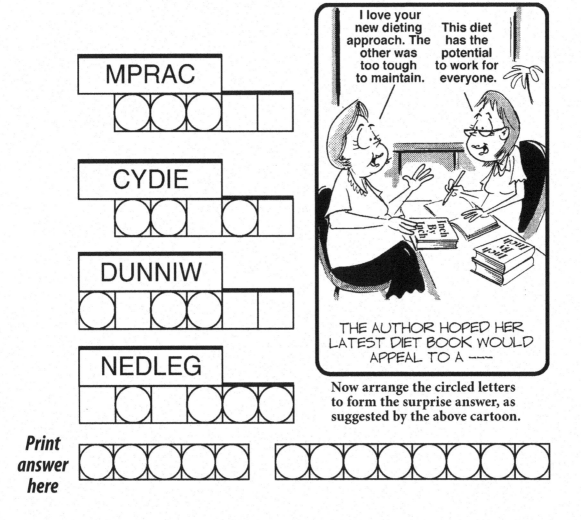

I love your new dieting approach. The other was too tough to maintain.

This diet has the potential to work for everyone.

THE AUTHOR HOPED HER LATEST DIET BOOK WOULD APPEAL TO A ----

Now arrange the circled letters
to form the surprise answer, as
suggested by the above cartoon.

Print
answer
here

JUMBLE®

Unscramble these four Jumbles, one letter to each square, to form four ordinary words.

SOPIE

HUDOG

YAPADY

COPIEL

I want to make sure my family is cared for.

The prudent strategy is to up your insurance as you make more.

HE THOUGHT THAT HAVING LIFE INSURANCE WAS A ----

Now arrange the circled letters to form the surprise answer, as suggested by the above cartoon.

Print answer here

JUMBLE®

Unscramble these four Jumbles, one letter to each square, to form four ordinary words.

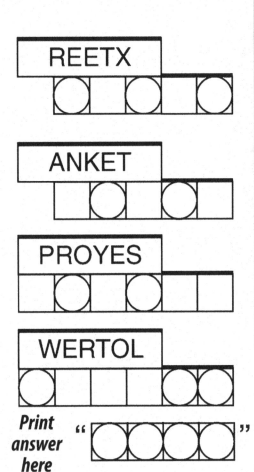

REETX

ANKET

PROYES

WERTOL

I have some of the only copies left of these movies.

Do you know what these are worth?

THE COLLECTOR OF CLASSIC FILMS OWNED ---

Now arrange the circled letters to form the surprise answer, as suggested by the above cartoon.

Print answer here

JUMBLE®

Unscramble these four Jumbles, one letter
to each square, to form four ordinary words.

POITV

MIRPP

SUDFEE

LETWAH

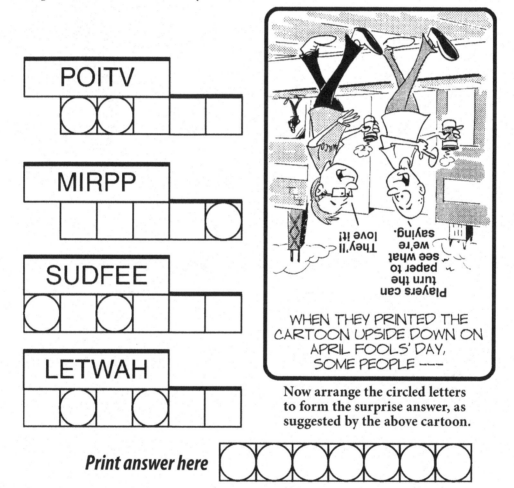

Players can
turn the
paper to
see what
we're
saying.

They'll
love it!

WHEN THEY PRINTED THE
CARTOON UPSIDE DOWN ON
APRIL FOOLS' DAY,
SOME PEOPLE ----

Now arrange the circled letters
to form the surprise answer, as
suggested by the above cartoon.

Print answer here

JUMBLE®

Unscramble these four Jumbles, one letter to each square, to form four ordinary words.

DEEGH

SIRYK

FEALNI

SUWINE

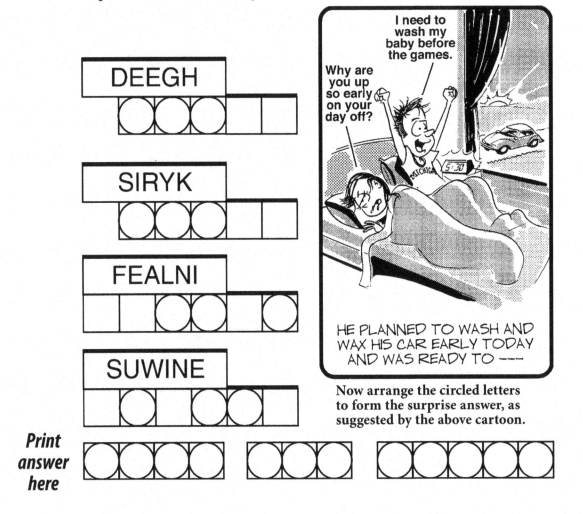

I need to wash my baby before the games.

Why are you up so early on your day off?

5:30

HE PLANNED TO WASH AND WAX HIS CAR EARLY TODAY AND WAS READY TO ---

Now arrange the circled letters to form the surprise answer, as suggested by the above cartoon.

Print answer here

JUMBLE.

Unscramble these four Jumbles, one letter to each square, to form four ordinary words.

RUYKM

SREDS

NAWMAL

APOITU

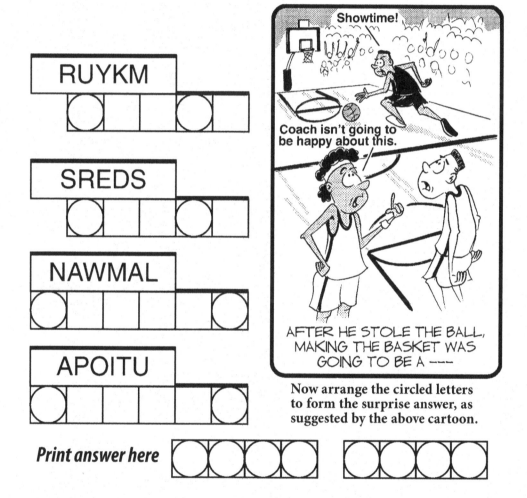

Showtime!

Coach isn't going to be happy about this.

AFTER HE STOLE THE BALL, MAKING THE BASKET WAS GOING TO BE A ---

Now arrange the circled letters to form the surprise answer, as suggested by the above cartoon.

Print answer here

JUMBLE®

Unscramble these four Jumbles, one letter
to each square, to form four ordinary words.

SUDEO

BEKOR

GAMEAD

FREEBO

How'd the No-Chin Hoyt Gang get in here?

AL CAPONE'S FAVORITE
RESTAURANT
WAS USUALLY ----

Now arrange the circled letters
to form the surprise answer, as
suggested by the above cartoon.

Print answer here

JUMBLE®

Unscramble these four Jumbles, one letter to each square, to form four ordinary words.

ELPXE

FRITD

DEETIC

ZULMEZ

How can we owe this much?

I thought they'd bill us later.

I ♥ JUMBLE

HIS HIGH CREDIT CARD BILL WAS A ----

Now arrange the circled letters to form the surprise answer, as suggested by the above cartoon.

Print answer here " ◯◯◯ - ◯◯◯ "

JUMBLE®

Unscramble these four Jumbles, one letter
to each square, to form four ordinary words.

TEPYT

VOEEK

MOSCUT

NIDTAY

Can't you do anything? I can't lift a thing without pain.

Why are you so stubborn? Why are you lifting? Beat it!

AFTER BEING SO RUDE TO THE DOCTOR, HE WAS ABOUT TO BECOME AN ----

Now arrange the circled letters
to form the surprise answer, as
suggested by the above cartoon.

Print
answer
here

◯◯◯ - ◯◯◯◯◯◯◯◯

JUMBLE®

Unscramble these four Jumbles, one letter
to each square, to form four ordinary words.

NOOZE

SMIPK

WHDERS

LOGIAE

WITH SO MANY CHILDREN
TRYING OUT THE EQUIPMENT,
THE NEW PLAYGROUND
HAD ---

Now arrange the circled letters
to form the surprise answer, as
suggested by the above cartoon.

**Print
answer
here**

JUMBLE®

Unscramble these four Jumbles, one letter to each square, to form four ordinary words.

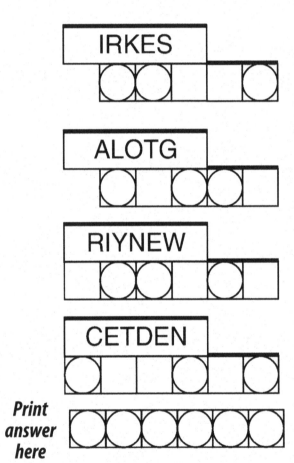

IRKES

ALOTG

RIYNEW

CETDEN

THE FOUR–STAR GENERAL OPENED HIS OWN RESTAURANT AND LOVED ――――

Now arrange the circled letters to form the surprise answer, as suggested by the above cartoon.

Print answer here

JUMBLE®

Unscramble these four Jumbles, one letter
to each square, to form four ordinary words.

DRENT

TORBO

OLLACE

KIYLLE

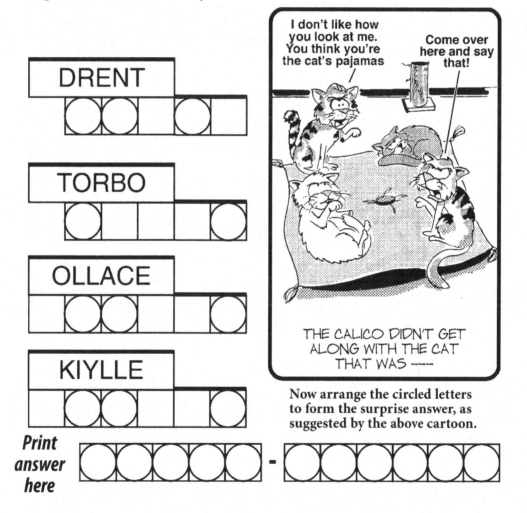

I don't like how
you look at me.
You think you're
the cat's pajamas

Come over
here and say
that!

THE CALICO DIDN'T GET
ALONG WITH THE CAT
THAT WAS ---

Now arrange the circled letters
to form the surprise answer, as
suggested by the above cartoon.

*Print
answer
here*

◯◯◯◯◯ - ◯◯◯◯◯◯

JUMBLE®

Unscramble these four Jumbles, one letter
to each square, to form four ordinary words.

OGGEU

KRAND

SLUDOH

CARIPY

I keep picking up
something on the mic.
What are you wearing?

My favorite
pants.
Why?

THE GUITARIST'S
FAVORITE PANTS
WERE ---

Now arrange the circled letters
to form the surprise answer, as
suggested by the above cartoon.

Print
answer
here

" ⃝⃝⃝⃝⃝⃝ - ⃝⃝⃝⃝⃝⃝ "

JUMBLE®

Unscramble these four Jumbles, one letter to each square, to form four ordinary words.

MEEEC

OEDGD

AABCSU

DOLYIB

I can't believe it Our home's lasted *this* long. a wreck.

THE BEAVERS' HOME HAD BEEN THERE FOR YEARS, BUT NOW IT WAS ----

Now arrange the circled letters to form the surprise answer, as suggested by the above cartoon.

Print answer here ◯◯◯ - ◯◯◯◯

JUMBLE®

Unscramble these four Jumbles, one letter to each square, to form four ordinary words.

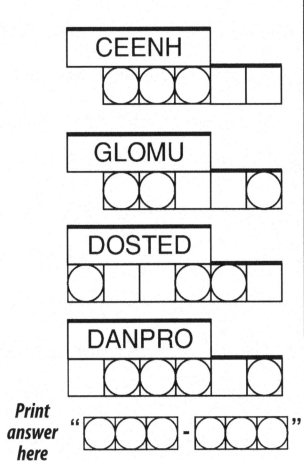

CEENH

GLOMU

DOSTED

DANPRO

THE MALE COLLEGE CHEERLEADERS' FAVORITE MEAL CONSISTED OF ----

Now arrange the circled letters to form the surprise answer, as suggested by the above cartoon.

Print answer here

" ⬡⬡⬡ - ⬡⬡⬡ " ⬡⬡⬡⬡⬡⬡⬡⬡

JUMBLE®

Unscramble these four Jumbles, one letter
to each square, to form four ordinary words.

BEIRB

CINEM

CCHITE

RUSPRE

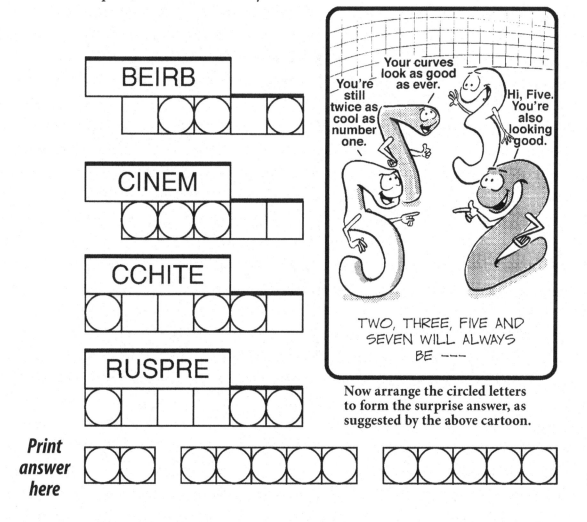

Your curves
look as good
as ever.

You're
still
twice as
cool as
number
one.

Hi, Five.
You're
also
looking
good.

TWO, THREE, FIVE AND
SEVEN WILL ALWAYS
BE — — —

Now arrange the circled letters
to form the surprise answer, as
suggested by the above cartoon.

*Print
answer
here*

JUMBLE®

Unscramble these four Jumbles, one letter to each square, to form four ordinary words.

XOYPE

DAYLM

GAUTOE

NARPYT

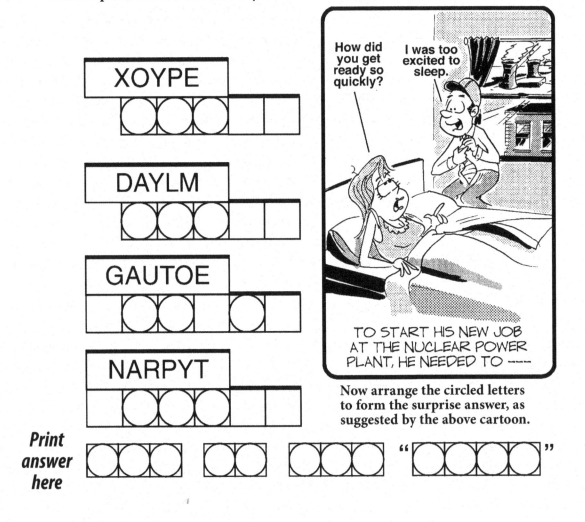

How did you get ready so quickly?

I was too excited to sleep.

TO START HIS NEW JOB AT THE NUCLEAR POWER PLANT, HE NEEDED TO ----

Now arrange the circled letters to form the surprise answer, as suggested by the above cartoon.

Print answer here

"   "

JUMBLE®

Unscramble these four Jumbles, one letter to each square, to form four ordinary words.

WARBL

NAGDL

CEAPIE

GIBEOL

Yes, I love my new phone. And it's waterproof! Sorry, I need to put you on hold.

THE CRANE LOVED HER NEW PHONE AND REALLY ENJOYED THE ----

Now arrange the circled letters to form the surprise answer, as suggested by the above cartoon.

Print answer here

" "

JUMBLE®

Unscramble these four Jumbles, one letter
to each square, to form four ordinary words.

TAIRO

GITDI

TAHYAP

SUIFEN

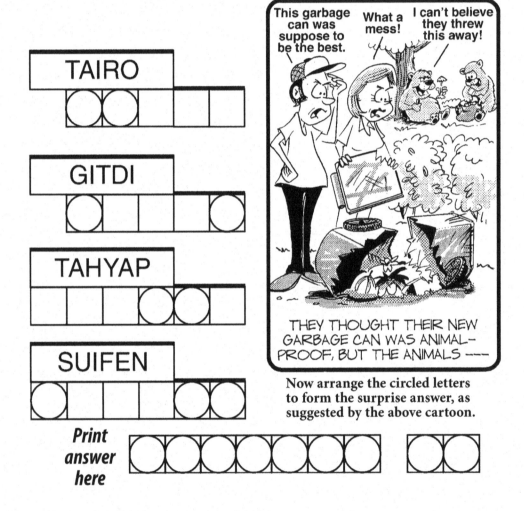

This garbage can was suppose to be the best.

What a mess!

I can't believe they threw this away!

THEY THOUGHT THEIR NEW GARBAGE CAN WAS ANIMAL-PROOF, BUT THE ANIMALS ----

Now arrange the circled letters to form the surprise answer, as suggested by the above cartoon.

Print
answer
here

JUMBLE®

Unscramble these four Jumbles, one letter to each square, to form four ordinary words.

EUKQA

TPYUT

SINITS

SUREUP

Wow! Where did you find grandma's Hummel figurines?

Vivian, get off that. It's very old.

Look at this toy, Mommy.

HER MOM'S SISTER HAD A LOT OF OLD FURNITURE, WHICH SHE CONSIDERED ----

Now arrange the circled letters to form the surprise answer, as suggested by the above cartoon.

Print answer here " ◯◯◯◯◯ - ◯◯◯◯◯ "

JUMBLE®

Unscramble these four Jumbles, one letter to each square, to form four ordinary words.

TLAME

TOHUM

BITBAR

LINDAS

You can't find your eggs!

Check under your bed.

I was sure I left them here.

THE HEN COULDN'T FIND HER EGGS AFTER SHE ----

Now arrange the circled letters to form the surprise answer, as suggested by the above cartoon.

Print answer here

JUMBLE®

Unscramble these four Jumbles, one letter to each square, to form four ordinary words.

GREEM

LATVE

WORDYS

PYNHEH

Weren't you going to make this today?

I forgot there was a playoff game on.

HER HUSBAND HAD MADE PLANS TO BUILD HER A NEW BOOKCASE TODAY, BUT HE ----

Now arrange the circled letters to form the surprise answer, as suggested by the above cartoon.

Print answer here

JUMBLE®

Unscramble these four Jumbles, one letter
to each square, to form four ordinary words.

TACEF

RATPA

MIFAYN

DOMELU

We did it! We paid more than the minimum and cut back. Here's the last payment!

It's really going to raise our credit score.

NOT CHARGING AS MUCH
ON THEIR
CREDIT CARDS ---

Now arrange the circled letters
to form the surprise answer, as
suggested by the above cartoon.

Print answer here ⟨⟩⟨⟩⟨⟩⟨⟩ ⟨⟩⟨⟩⟨⟩

JUMBLE®

Unscramble these four Jumbles, one letter
to each square, to form four ordinary words.

SMOPT

ORFPO

INCOCI

LAUNAN

*Print
answer
here*

You are late more than
40 % of the time and
your class failed
85 % of the time...

Is there
much more?

THE MATH TEACHER WAS
BEING REPRIMANDED
BECAUSE OF HIS ———

Now arrange the circled letters
to form the surprise answer, as
suggested by the above cartoon.

JUMBLE®

Unscramble these four Jumbles, one letter to each square, to form four ordinary words.

SOYBS

LIXEE

LUDTON

WHERDS

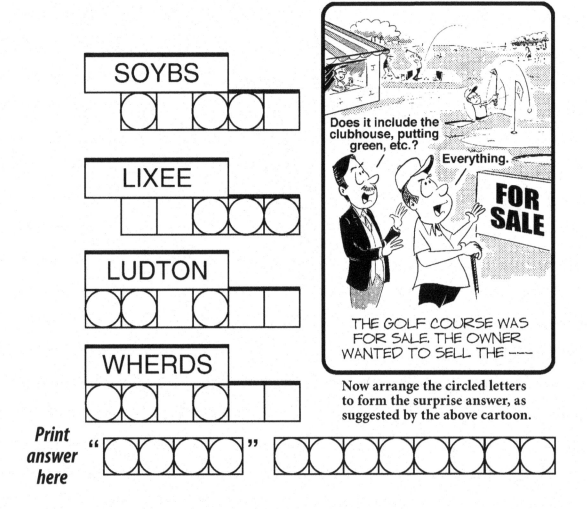

Does it include the clubhouse, putting green, etc.?

Everything.

FOR SALE

THE GOLF COURSE WAS FOR SALE. THE OWNER WANTED TO SELL THE ----

Now arrange the circled letters to form the surprise answer, as suggested by the above cartoon.

Print answer here " ⬡⬡⬡⬡ " ⬡⬡⬡⬡⬡⬡⬡⬡⬡

JUMBLE®

Unscramble these four Jumbles, one letter
to each square, to form four ordinary words.

SUGES

ONYEM

LLOWYS

ANNLID

Why keep just the dictionary cover?

Beats me. I'm at a loss for words.

OWNING A DICTIONARY
WITHOUT PAGES IS ---

Now arrange the circled letters
to form the surprise answer, as
suggested by the above cartoon.

Print
answer
here

JUMBLE®

Unscramble these four Jumbles, one letter
to each square, to form four ordinary words.

RAWRO

FOLYT

NORLEG

LAPTEL

No practice
until you
feel better.

But my
team
needs
me.

SICK IN BED, MOM
WOULDN'T LET HIM
GO TO PRACTICE UNTIL
HE COULD ---

Now arrange the circled letters
to form the surprise answer, as
suggested by the above cartoon.

Print answer here

JUMBLE®

Unscramble these four Jumbles, one letter
to each square, to form four ordinary words.

NYDIW

LOAAK

DOSMET

TRYEAR

Print answer here

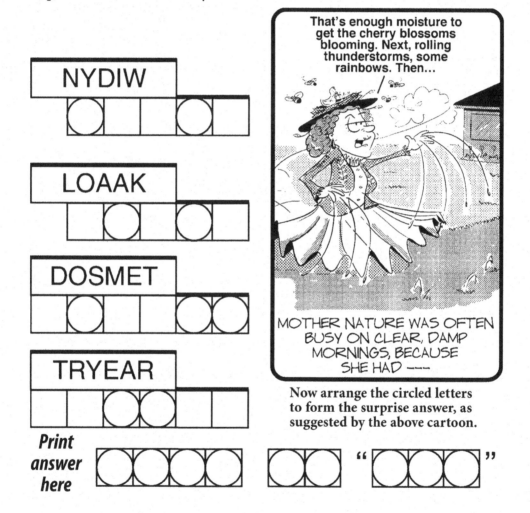

That's enough moisture to
get the cherry blossoms
blooming. Next, rolling
thunderstorms, some
rainbows. Then...

MOTHER NATURE WAS OFTEN
BUSY ON CLEAR, DAMP
MORNINGS, BECAUSE
SHE HAD ----

Now arrange the circled letters
to form the surprise answer, as
suggested by the above cartoon.

" "

JUMBLE®

Unscramble these four Jumbles, one letter to each square, to form four ordinary words.

DADED

CINEW

DIHNED

MINEUM

Here's to a night out with the family.

I may need another glass.

I can't believe I forgot my phone.

Yuck! This is gross.

WHEN THE KIDS COMPLAINED AT DINNER, THEIR PARENTS WERE BEING ---

Now arrange the circled letters to form the surprise answer, as suggested by the above cartoon.

Print answer here " ⬡⬡⬡⬡⬡⬡ " AND ⬡⬡⬡⬡⬡

JUMBLE®

Unscramble these four Jumbles, one letter to each square, to form four ordinary words.

ODWUN

RYBUL

GEVNOR

SONEOL

You did it!

I can't believe this!

AFTER ROLLING 12 STRIKES IN A ROW FOR A 300, HE WAS ----

Now arrange the circled letters to form the surprise answer, as suggested by the above cartoon.

Print answer here

JUMBLE®

Unscramble these four Jumbles, one letter
to each square, to form four ordinary words.

RAWEF

OTHIS

GWILEG

ONTRYH

Are you coming, Bob?

What do you say? Everyone's going.

Okay.

HE DIDN'T WANT
TO GO TUBING,
BUT HE DID TO ----

Now arrange the circled letters
to form the surprise answer, as
suggested by the above cartoon.

*Print
answer
here*

JUMBLE.

Unscramble these four Jumbles, one letter to each square, to form four ordinary words.

KAHYS

NORDF

DEDARM

CRONEE

You're doing well, given your injuries.

I was lucky, but I think of those we lost every day.

IN MEMORY FOR ALL THOSE LOST

DOCTORS AT VETERANS' HOSPITALS DEDICATE THEIR LIVES TO TREATING THE ----

Now arrange the circled letters to form the surprise answer, as suggested by the above cartoon.

Print answer here

" ⬡⬡⬡⬡⬡⬡ "   ⬡⬡⬡⬡⬡⬡

JUMBLE®

Unscramble these four Jumbles, one letter to each square, to form four ordinary words.

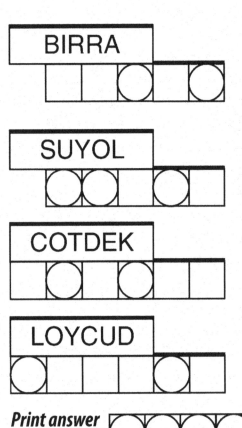

BIRRA

SUYOL

COTDEK

LOYCUD

We can count on each other like we count on the sunrise.

Yeah, you've got the sun, you've got the moon, and you've got the Rolling Stones.

THE ROLLING STONES HAVE BEEN TOGETHER SO LONG, BECAUSE, AS A GROUP, THEY ARE ---

Now arrange the circled letters to form the surprise answer, as suggested by the above cartoon.

Print answer here

JUMBLE®

Unscramble these four Jumbles, one letter
to each square, to form four ordinary words.

GEFDU

BOYBH

MOOTTB

MARIDE

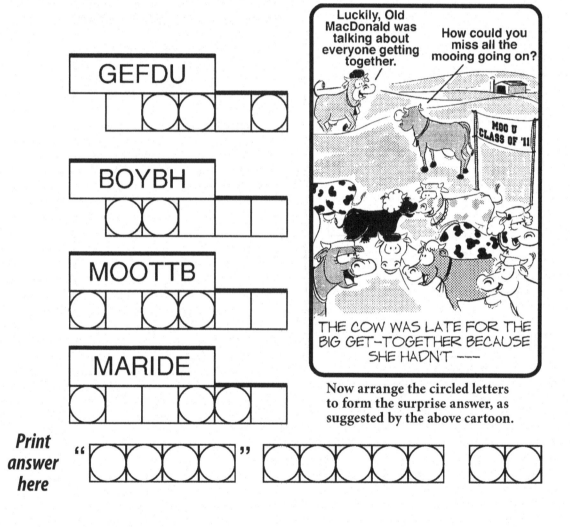

Luckily, Old MacDonald was talking about everyone getting together.

How could you miss all the mooing going on?

MOO U CLASS OF '11

THE COW WAS LATE FOR THE
BIG GET-TOGETHER BECAUSE
SHE HADN'T ----

Now arrange the circled letters
to form the surprise answer, as
suggested by the above cartoon.

Print
answer
here

" ⃝⃝⃝⃝ " ⃝⃝⃝⃝⃝ ⃝⃝

JUMBLE®

Unscramble these four Jumbles, one letter to each square, to form four ordinary words.

LEYNW

THIWD

FLUNEG

TOMIRP

I wanted to play it safe and decided not to go for three.

Good for you.

HE TOOK THE DOUBLE, MAYBE HE COULD HAVE TRIPLED, BUT HE DIDN'T WANT TO ---

Now arrange the circled letters to form the surprise answer, as suggested by the above cartoon.

Print answer here

JUMBLE®

Unscramble these four Jumbles, one letter
to each square, to form four ordinary words.

RIDYT

NOYHE

AYYDPA

TUDILE

You were great in "Risky Business." No wonder you got this job.

Taking flying lessons didn't hurt. Action!

"MAVERICK"

TOM CRUISE PLAYED
A PILOT IN "TOP GUN"
AFTER HE ----

Now arrange the circled letters
to form the surprise answer, as
suggested by the above cartoon.

Print answer here

JUMBLE®

Unscramble these four Jumbles, one letter to each square, to form four ordinary words.

YILVN

TABYT

SEODUX

TUCLAA

So what do you think? Want to buy it?

I love it!

WHEN ASKED IF HE LIKED THE NEW FOUR-STRINGED INSTRUMENT, HE SAID THIS.

Now arrange the circled letters to form the surprise answer, as suggested by the above cartoon.

Print answer here

" ⬡⬡⬡⬡ - ⬡⬡⬡⬡ - ⬡⬡ "

JUMBLE®

Unscramble these four Jumbles, one letter to each square, to form four ordinary words.

CABHE

OTAPI

MABLGE

BMACEE

Wow! Look at all those houses you've built.

I want to show future customers my portfolio.

WELCOME to RAY'S CONSTRUCTION
*Floor Plans
*Contact
*About

THE CONTRACTOR WANTED TO BUILD MORE HOUSES, SO HE BUILT A ----

Now arrange the circled letters to form the surprise answer, as suggested by the above cartoon.

Print answer here ◯◯◯◯ ◯◯◯◯

JUMBLE®

Unscramble these four Jumbles, one letter
to each square, to form four ordinary words.

HICTP

EGAVU

ADIRUS

CUDNIT

I can't believe
your little girl is
getting married.
Are you doing
okay?

I'm so happy
for her. But I
also miss my
little girl.

WHEN THE BAKER MADE A
WEDDING CAKE FOR HIS
DAUGHTER, HE WAS ----

Now arrange the circled letters
to form the surprise answer, as
suggested by the above cartoon.

**Print
answer
here**

"◯◯◯◯◯◯◯" ◯◯

JUMBLE®

Unscramble these four Jumbles, one letter
to each square, to form four ordinary words.

ZALEG

USEIS

QIYETU

FARLVO

Wow, Father.
You never miss
a workout, do
you?

Nope. I'm here
every day after
morning service.

THE PRIEST TOOK HIS
WORKOUT ROUTINE VERY
SERIOUSLY AND WENT TO
THE GYM —

Now arrange the circled letters
to form the surprise answer, as
suggested by the above cartoon.

*Print
answer
here*

JUMBLE®

Unscramble these four Jumbles, one letter
to each square, to form four ordinary words.

SYPHU

DURFA

NERROY

ITOXCE

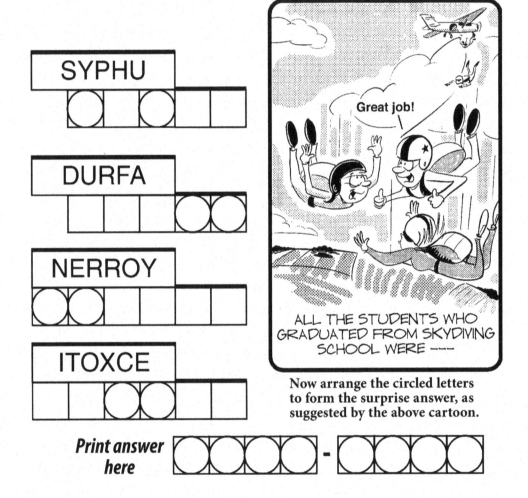

Great job!

ALL THE STUDENTS WHO
GRADUATED FROM SKYDIVING
SCHOOL WERE ----

Now arrange the circled letters
to form the surprise answer, as
suggested by the above cartoon.

**Print answer
here** ◯◯◯◯ - ◯◯◯◯

JUMBLE®

Unscramble these four Jumbles, one letter to each square, to form four ordinary words.

CITYH

SONOW

LIEEDY

NEDTAT

There he goes.

Nothing slows him down.

SLEEPY HOLLOW'S HORSEMAN MAINTAINED HIS SPEED IN SPITE OF THE ----

Now arrange the circled letters to form the surprise answer, as suggested by the above cartoon.

Print answer here

JUMBLE®

Unscramble these four Jumbles, one letter to each square, to form four ordinary words.

TUNYT

KUNYF

REPDAA

XTREEP

This 1955 doubled die cent is very rare. It's yours for $2,000.

It's a beauty!

HEADS OR TAILS Coin Shop

THE RARE LINCOLN ONE-CENT COIN COST A ---

Now arrange the circled letters to form the surprise answer, as suggested by the above cartoon.

Print answer here

JUMBLE®

Unscramble these four Jumbles, one letter to each square, to form four ordinary words.

NOINO

YAKKA

DAMOWE

SAWCEH

Look! I got him. This is great!

Looks like I have a new fishing buddy.

AFTER GOING FISHING FOR THE FIRST TIME, HE WAS ———

Now arrange the circled letters to form the surprise answer, as suggested by the above cartoon.

Print answer here

129

JUMBLE®

Unscramble these four Jumbles, one letter
to each square, to form four ordinary words.

HOVCU

FOREY

TAYNLE

INEFIT

Can I borrow your dress? I'd really appreciate it.

No. You left a stain on my dress the last time.

SHE ASKED HER SISTER IF SHE COULD BORROW A DRESS, BUT HER SISTER WASN'T ----

Now arrange the circled letters
to form the surprise answer, as
suggested by the above cartoon.

Print
answer
here

JUMBLE®

Unscramble these four Jumbles, one letter to each square, to form four ordinary words.

HELWE

GLICO

MULSAY

XFINUL

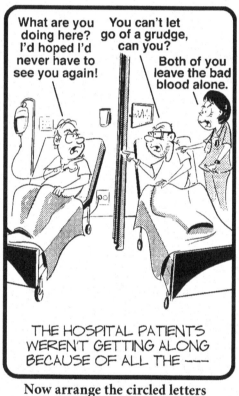

What are you doing here? I'd hoped I'd never have to see you again!

You can't let go of a grudge, can you?

Both of you leave the bad blood alone.

THE HOSPITAL PATIENTS WEREN'T GETTING ALONG BECAUSE OF ALL THE ---

Now arrange the circled letters to form the surprise answer, as suggested by the above cartoon.

Print answer here

JUMBLE®

Unscramble these four Jumbles, one letter
to each square, to form four ordinary words.

BADIE

BUGOM

RERACE

SYAART

As for fog, it'll depend on cloud coverage and where you live. Calm winds will also play a part.

Springfield

Shelbyville

Capital City

HOW WIDESPREAD WOULD THE FOG BE TOMORROW MORNING? IT WAS A BIT OF A ---

Now arrange the circled letters to form the surprise answer, as suggested by the above cartoon.

Print answer here

JUMBLE®

Unscramble these four Jumbles, one letter to each square, to form four ordinary words.

CYMRE

UNEVE

NANFIT

GLUEED

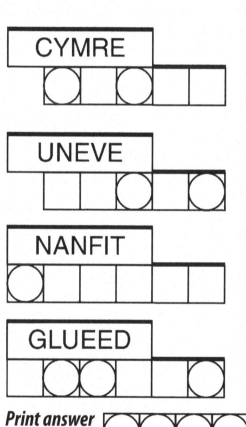

They've been coming all day to play!

THE CASINO PUT IN NEW SLOTS TO ATTRACT CUSTOMERS AND WAS ABLE TO ———

Now arrange the circled letters to form the surprise answer, as suggested by the above cartoon.

Print answer here

 '

JUMBLE®

Unscramble these four Jumbles, one letter to each square, to form four ordinary words.

BURYG

SODUE

NEYOLP

CFEETD

So, what do you think, Mr. Hoyt? Are they up to your standards?

Let's see. "The Jumble artist knew where to DRAW THE LINE." I'd reword that. Also...

Nice one.

THE JUMBLE AUTHOR'S NEW APPRENTICE WAS HAPPY TO BE THE ----

Now arrange the circled letters to form the surprise answer, as suggested by the above cartoon.

Print answer here " "

JUMBLE®

Unscramble these four Jumbles, one letter to each square, to form four ordinary words.

SUTGE

ALQEU

SOTFRY

GHUATT

I'm glad he gave up boxing. He's the most powerful hitter I've seen.

He really knocks it out of here!

THE BOXER WHO BECAME A BASEBALL PLAYER WAS A ———

Now arrange the circled letters to form the surprise answer, as suggested by the above cartoon.

Print answer here

JUMBLE®

Unscramble these four Jumbles, one letter to each square, to form four ordinary words.

PEMTT

AUTOQ

CINRIO

CAUVMU

He won't listen. It's like I'm invisible. And when I asked for a raise, he laughed.

Time to stop complaining and do something.

HE COMPLAINED ABOUT HIS JOB INCESSANTLY. HIS WIFE TOLD HIM TO ----

Now arrange the circled letters to form the surprise answer, as suggested by the above cartoon.

Print answer here

JUMBLE®

Unscramble these four Jumbles, one letter
to each square, to form four ordinary words.

LIDAV

SLACH

GRANDO

COTPEK

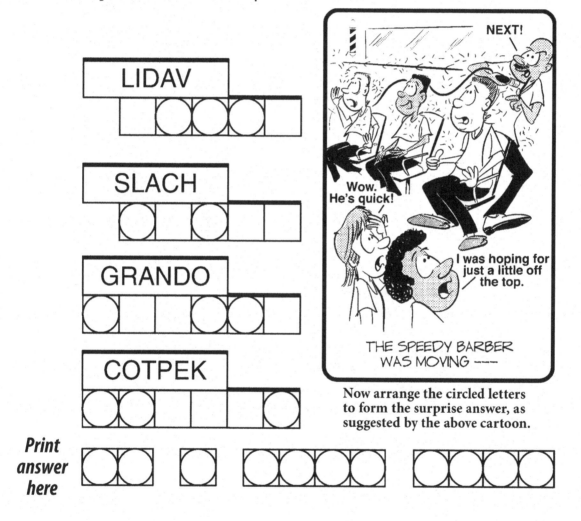

NEXT!

Wow.
He's quick!

I was hoping for
just a little off
the top.

THE SPEEDY BARBER
WAS MOVING ----

Now arrange the circled letters
to form the surprise answer, as
suggested by the above cartoon.

*Print
answer
here*

JUMBLE®

Unscramble these four Jumbles, one letter
to each square, to form four ordinary words.

CAKAB

NARDB

TEEKLT

AJVILO

I'm lucky you came along. I didn't know how I was going to get the car off the ground.

It's what I do.

THE BUNNY HAD A PROBLEM CHANGING THE FLAT. THANKFULLY, HE COULD CALL A ---

Now arrange the circled letters
to form the surprise answer, as
suggested by the above cartoon.

Print
answer
here

JUMBLE®

Unscramble these four Jumbles, one letter to each square, to form four ordinary words.

ATVIL

OYARN

OBEWLB

EDDGER

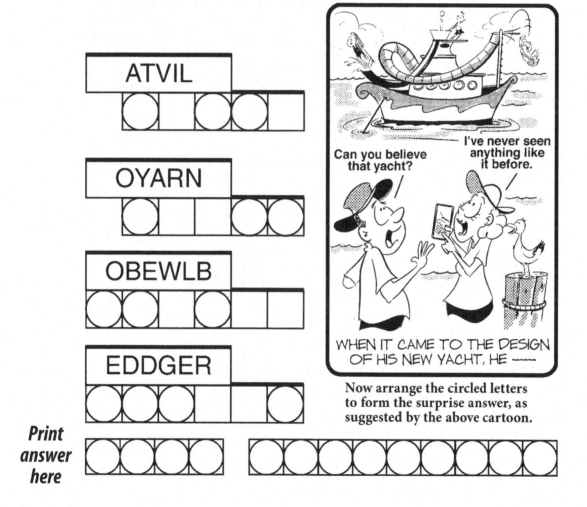

Can you believe that yacht?

I've never seen anything like it before.

WHEN IT CAME TO THE DESIGN OF HIS NEW YACHT, HE ----

Now arrange the circled letters to form the surprise answer, as suggested by the above cartoon.

Print answer here

JUMBLE®

Unscramble these four Jumbles, one letter
to each square, to form four ordinary words.

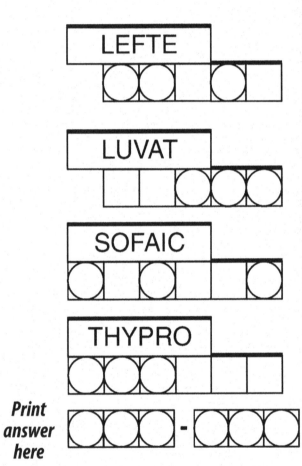

LEFTE

LUVAT

SOFAIC

THYPRO

TO MAKE THE TRIPLE PLAY,
THE DEFENSE
NEEDED AN ---

Now arrange the circled letters
to form the surprise answer, as
suggested by the above cartoon.

Print
answer
here

JUMBLE®

Unscramble these four Jumbles, one letter
to each square, to form four ordinary words.

FINSF

NOIYR

RELENK

IGNNNI

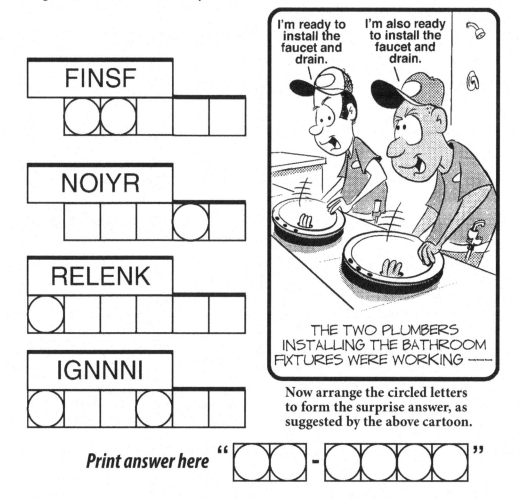

I'm ready to install the faucet and drain.

I'm also ready to install the faucet and drain.

THE TWO PLUMBERS
INSTALLING THE BATHROOM
FIXTURES WERE WORKING ----

Now arrange the circled letters
to form the surprise answer, as
suggested by the above cartoon.

Print answer here " ⬭⬭ - ⬭⬭⬭⬭ "

JUMBLE®

Unscramble these four Jumbles, one letter to each square, to form four ordinary words.

DEGAA

GEJDU

TINKTE

HNPEYH

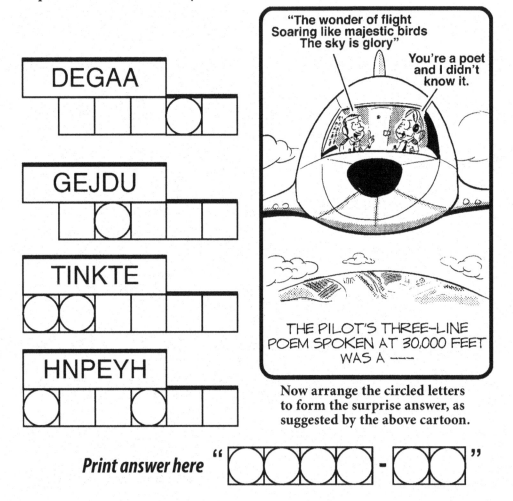

"The wonder of flight
Soaring like majestic birds
The sky is glory"

You're a poet
and I didn't
know it.

THE PILOT'S THREE-LINE
POEM SPOKEN AT 30,000 FEET
WAS A ---

Now arrange the circled letters to form the surprise answer, as suggested by the above cartoon.

Print answer here " ⃝⃝⃝⃝ - ⃝⃝ "

JUMBLE®

Unscramble these four Jumbles, one letter
to each square, to form four ordinary words.

HLIEW

LRUBB

RATEHH

FRIDTA

If you knew how
to play, we'd have
taken them all.

Why
would
you try
for a
slam?

I wish
they'd
leave.

THE BRIDGE PAIR
ARGUED CONSTANTLY,
SO THEIR OPPONENTS
HOPED THEY'D ―――

Now arrange the circled letters
to form the surprise answer, as
suggested by the above cartoon.

*Print
answer
here*

JUMBLE®

Unscramble these four Jumbles, one letter to each square, to form four ordinary words.

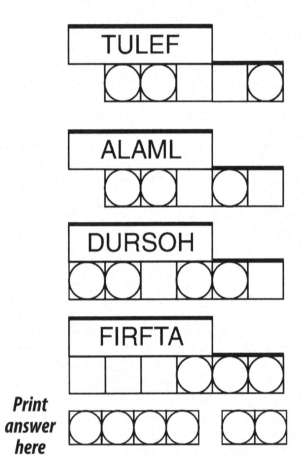

TULEF

ALAML

DURSOH

FIRFTA

Chef, would you like to try my dish?

I only eat my own creations. Save your dish for the kids' menu.

THE CHEF WHO WOULDN'T TRY FOOD PREPARED BY OTHER CHEFS WAS ———

Now arrange the circled letters to form the surprise answer, as suggested by the above cartoon.

Print answer here

JUMBLE®

Unscramble these four Jumbles, one letter
to each square, to form four ordinary words.

DEMMO

RIENL

THOMOS

RARUYQ

I don't understand.
Your poems are
becoming popular.

Why
would
you
quit?

I don't
know. I'm
just over it.

THE POET JUST QUIT. SHE
STOPPED WRITING POETRY.
THERE WAS NO ---

Now arrange the circled letters
to form the surprise answer, as
suggested by the above cartoon.

**Print
answer
here**

JUMBLE®

Unscramble these four Jumbles, one letter to each square, to form four ordinary words.

TOBHO

LETKN

SERYDS

YOUPAT

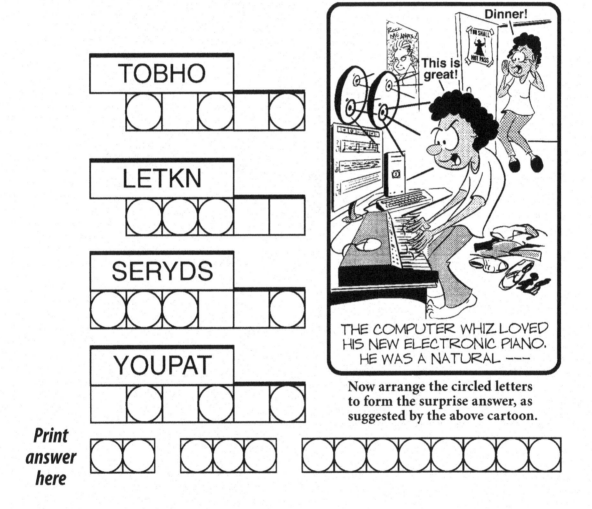

Dinner!

This is great!

THE COMPUTER WHIZ LOVED HIS NEW ELECTRONIC PIANO. HE WAS A NATURAL ---

Now arrange the circled letters to form the surprise answer, as suggested by the above cartoon.

Print answer here

JUMBLE®

Unscramble these four Jumbles, one letter to each square, to form four ordinary words.

DENYE

SSUHL

SOWDRY

SCAAVN

Kids! It's noon. Time to eat.

After one more ace.

He wishes.

THE TENNIS PLAYERS STOPPED PLAYING WHEN ----

Now arrange the circled letters to form the surprise answer, as suggested by the above cartoon.

Print answer here

JUMBLE®

Unscramble these four Jumbles, one letter to each square, to form four ordinary words.

GHURS

SAYID

GOOTRF

TAVCIE

THE CEMETERY'S NEW SECURITY GUARD WORKED THE ----

Now arrange the circled letters to form the surprise answer, as suggested by the above cartoon.

Print answer here

JUMBLE®

Unscramble these four Jumbles, one letter
to each square, to form four ordinary words.

VADIO

WORLG

LIFTEL

VONBIE

Look! Our foliage is coming back.

I'm so glad winter is over.

WITH WINTER OVER, SPRING
WAS THIS TO THE TREES.

Now arrange the circled letters
to form the surprise answer, as
suggested by the above cartoon.

Print answer here A " ⬭⬭ - ⬭⬭⬭⬭ "

JUMBLE®

Unscramble these four Jumbles, one letter
to each square, to form four ordinary words.

WORNC

PAZTO

XDECEE

SPYMIK

Let's go up
an octave on
"Do you need
anybody?"

Sounds good.
I have to
admit it's
getting better.

THEY WORKED ON
THE SONG SEPARATELY,
AND THEN ---

Now arrange the circled letters
to form the surprise answer, as
suggested by the above cartoon.

Print
answer
here

JUMBLE®

Unscramble these four Jumbles, one letter to each square, to form four ordinary words.

DOMUN

SWNHO

TIMSAG

PONCAY

It's only 1972. I'm sure there'll be thousands of people living up here by the 1990s, 2001 at the latest.

Or sooner.

THE LAST TIME HUMANS WALKED ON THE LUNAR SURFACE, IT WAS ---

Now arrange the circled letters to form the surprise answer, as suggested by the above cartoon.

Print answer here

JUMBLE®

Unscramble these four Jumbles, one letter to each square, to form four ordinary words.

NUGTR

SEYMS

CKRIYT

PIDEME

Hey, kids! Winter's over. Time to take your toys and play outside.

WHEN CHILDREN PLAYED WITH THEIR NEW SLINKY TOYS IN APRIL OF 1946, IT WAS ——

Now arrange the circled letters to form the surprise answer, as suggested by the above cartoon.

Print answer here

JUMBLE®

Unscramble these four Jumbles, one letter
to each square, to form four ordinary words.

VONLE

MUPEL

ZEESEN

TROFAM

More
Champagne?

All this? And
can you
believe the
view?

I love
it!

THE ELEGANT NEW BOX SEATS
AT THE BASEBALL STADIUM
WERE ---

Now arrange the circled letters
to form the surprise answer, as
suggested by the above cartoon.

Print answer here " ◯◯◯ - ◯◯◯ "

JUMBLE®

Unscramble these four Jumbles, one letter
to each square, to form four ordinary words.

PLOEE

CIRKB

TARREH

DUPIMO

THE CHEMISTS ATE
LUNCH EVERY DAY
AT THE ----

Now arrange the circled letters
to form the surprise answer, as
suggested by the above cartoon.

Print
answer
here

JUMBLE®

Unscramble these four Jumbles, one letter to each square, to form four ordinary words.

SNIYH

CCOLK

AMTENG

ARQUES

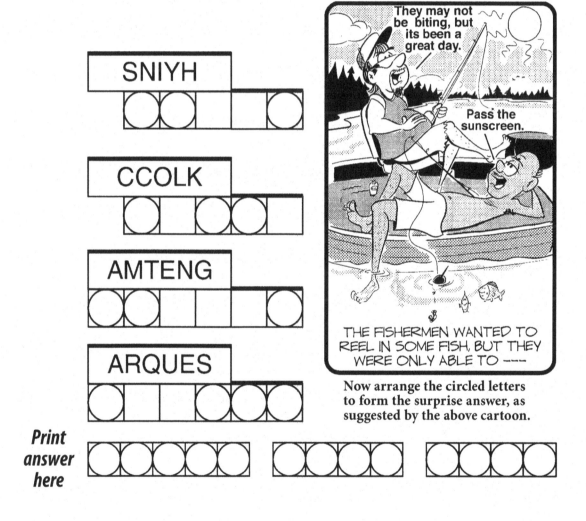

They may not be biting, but its been a great day.

Pass the sunscreen.

THE FISHERMEN WANTED TO REEL IN SOME FISH, BUT THEY WERE ONLY ABLE TO ----

Now arrange the circled letters to form the surprise answer, as suggested by the above cartoon.

Print answer here

JUMBLE®

Unscramble these four Jumbles, one letter
to each square, to form four ordinary words.

TALOG

MEPLI

DUNEDS

RUBSAD

These symbols show musicians what to play.

This is extraordinary!

WHEN THEY FIGURED OUT HOW
TO WRITE DOWN MUSIC,
IT WAS ----

Now arrange the circled letters
to form the surprise answer, as
suggested by the above cartoon.

Print answer here

JUMBLE®

Unscramble these four Jumbles, one letter
to each square, to form four ordinary words.

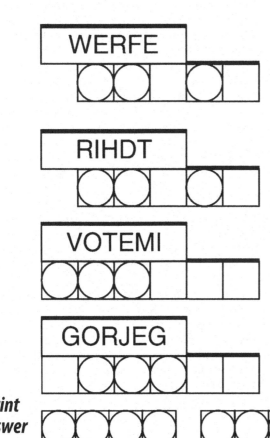

WERFE

RIHDT

VOTEMI

GORJEG

People love it.
Green means proceed,
red means stop.

Amazing!

THE FIRST TRAFFIC LIGHT
EVER INSTALLED
WAS POPULAR ----

Now arrange the circled letters
to form the surprise answer, as
suggested by the above cartoon.

*Print
answer
here*

◯◯◯◯ ◯◯◯ ◯◯◯-◯◯

JUMBLE®

Unscramble these four Jumbles, one letter to each square, to form four ordinary words.

RACYR

OBATO

LENKIU

MTRWAH

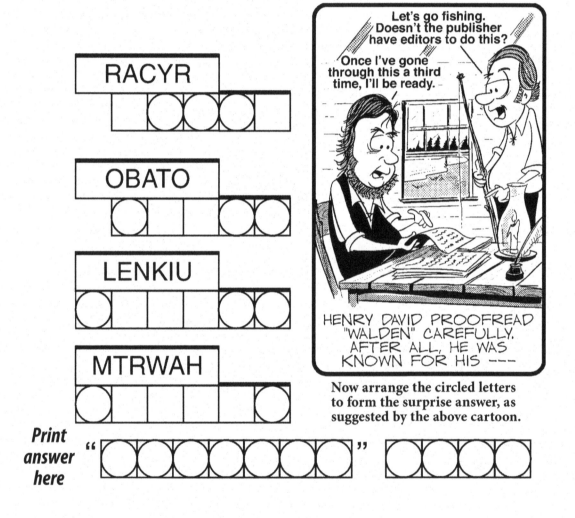

Let's go fishing. Doesn't the publisher have editors to do this?

Once I've gone through this a third time, I'll be ready.

HENRY DAVID PROOFREAD "WALDEN" CAREFULLY. AFTER ALL, HE WAS KNOWN FOR HIS ---

Now arrange the circled letters to form the surprise answer, as suggested by the above cartoon.

Print answer here "⬡⬡⬡⬡⬡⬡⬡" ⬡⬡⬡⬡

JUMBLE®

Unscramble these four Jumbles, one letter to each square, to form four ordinary words.

LAWOL

LAHEV

YUKRET

FARYDT

We finally caught you.

I can't believe it! I thought I'd never get caught.

I don't think so.

FOR THE PURSE-SNATCHER, GETTING CAUGHT WAS ---

Now arrange the circled letters to form the surprise answer, as suggested by the above cartoon.

Print answer here

JUMBLE.

Unscramble these four Jumbles, one letter
to each square, to form four ordinary words.

HNOYE

BTORI

KAWENE

VACRIA

How could they blow that lead?

What kind of throw was that?

Come on!

AFTER WATCHING THEIR TEAM
BLOW A HUGE LEAD, THE BEER
PUB TURNED INTO A ----

Now arrange the circled letters
to form the surprise answer, as
suggested by the above cartoon.

*Print answer
here*   "◯◯◯◯◯" ◯◯◯

JUMBLE®

Unscramble these four Jumbles, one letter
to each square, to form four ordinary words.

XTREE

VAHNE

HTORYP

MYSLOB

Nice Slices

Oven Lovin

Opening Soon

Wow! Another
business
opening.

A bakery right
there will
complement
our meats and
cheeses nicely.

THEIR BUSINESS WAS ON
A STREET WITH MANY
SHOPS AND ANOTHER
ONE WAS OPENING ---

Now arrange the circled letters
to form the surprise answer, as
suggested by the above cartoon.

**Print
answer
here**

⬡⬡⬡⬡ "⬡⬡⬡⬡⬡"

JUMBLE®

Unscramble these four Jumbles, one letter to each square, to form four ordinary words.

LEWNY

FURGF

DEBNOY

ZLAREB

THE NEW EMPLOYEE AT THE NUCLEAR POWER PLANT WAS A ———

Now arrange the circled letters to form the surprise answer, as suggested by the above cartoon.

Print answer here

JUMBLE Ever After

Challenger Puzzles

JUMBLE®

Unscramble these six Jumbles, one letter
to each square, to form six ordinary words.

FLUTIE

TILPUF

RIMPER

CEVIED

HAWRTT

INDOOM

WHY ATLAS WAS
ARRESTED.

Now arrange the circled letters
to form the surprise answer, as
suggested by the above cartoon.

*Print answer
here*   HE ⬜⬜⬜⬜⬜ ⬜⬜ THE ⬜⬜⬜⬜⬜

JUMBLE®

Unscramble these six Jumbles, one letter
to each square, to form six ordinary words.

GINTRY

BOALIN

RUBBUS

FREBLY

TELLMA

CEDITE

A MAN WHO LIKES
YOU TO BE AT HIS
SERVICE.

Now arrange the circled letters
to form the surprise answer, as
suggested by the above cartoon.

Print answer here THE ◯◯◯◯◯◯◯◯◯

JUMBLE®

Unscramble these six Jumbles, one letter to each square, to form six ordinary words.

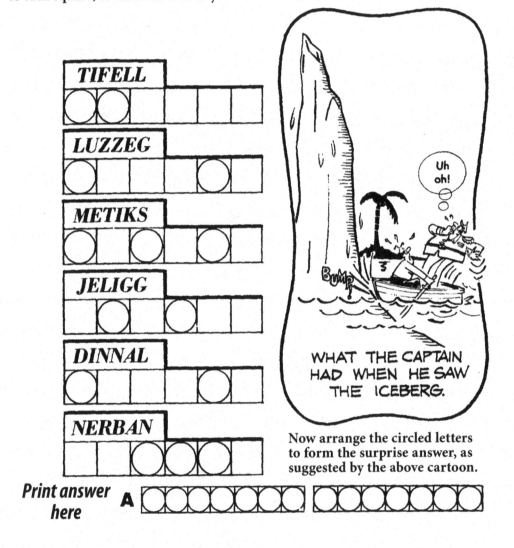

TIFELL

LUZZEG

METIKS

JELIGG

DINNAL

NERBAN

WHAT THE CAPTAIN HAD WHEN HE SAW THE ICEBERG.

Now arrange the circled letters to form the surprise answer, as suggested by the above cartoon.

Print answer here A

166

JUMBLE®

Unscramble these six Jumbles, one letter to each square, to form six ordinary words.

DARAPE

MUNCOL

TABMIG

DUBOYE

GLANID

SHARTH

LONDON AIRPORT

By Jove! Hardly recognized him

HOW HE RETURNED HOME FROM A VACATION AT A GAMBLING RESORT.

Now arrange the circled letters to form the surprise answer, as suggested by the above cartoon.

Print answer here

JUMBLE®

Unscramble these six Jumbles, one letter
to each square, to form six ordinary words.

SHABIN

COSTAM

YADDLE

ARUSSE

NAUGIA

TILBEG

He must
know
PLENTY!

But he
won't
talk!

Next!

WHAT THEY SAID
ABOUT THE
PSYCHIATRIST.

Now arrange the circled letters
to form the surprise answer, as
suggested by the above cartoon.

**Print answer
here** ◯◯◯◯◯'◯ **HIS** ◯◯◯◯◯◯◯◯◯

Print answer here

168

JUMBLE.

Unscramble these six Jumbles, one letter
to each square, to form six ordinary words.

BRAYNE

REMAID

FLEMUF

DORPAY

NITTAC

MEHRAM

WHAT YOU MIGHT
EAT AT A
BUFFET DINNER.

Now arrange the circled letters
to form the surprise answer, as
suggested by the above cartoon.

Print
answer
here
A " ⃝⃝⃝⃝⃝⃝⃝⃝ " ⃝⃝⃝⃝

JUMBLE®

Unscramble these six Jumbles, one letter
to each square, to form six ordinary words.

LAPEAT

DRAHLY

RANLEY

PAYNOC

ZEMENY

REVUIQ

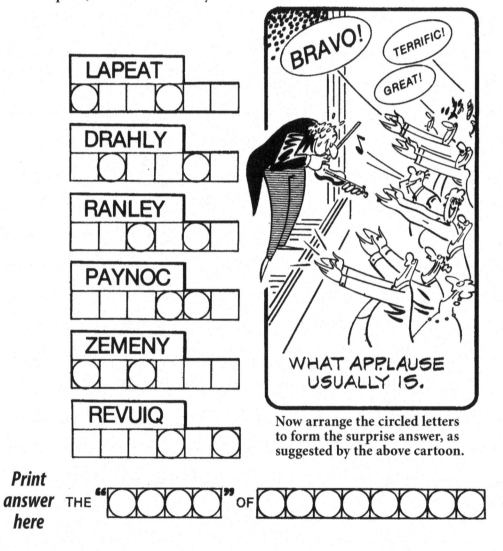

BRAVO!

TERRIFIC!

GREAT!

WHAT APPLAUSE
USUALLY IS.

Now arrange the circled letters
to form the surprise answer, as
suggested by the above cartoon.

*Print
answer
here*   THE "⟨◯◯◯◯◯⟩" OF ⟨◯◯◯◯◯◯◯◯◯◯⟩

JUMBLE®

Unscramble these six Jumbles, one letter
to each square, to form six ordinary words.

FLUEYE

TUBECK

CITOXE

INQUAT

INGLEM

NESSUC

Mind moving
your feet,
dear?

WHAT A BIG NOISE
AT THE OFFICE
OFTEN IS AT HOME.

Now arrange the circled letters
to form the surprise answer, as
suggested by the above cartoon.

Print
answer
here

A

JUMBLE®

Unscramble these six Jumbles, one letter
to each square, to form six ordinary words.

TELKIN

DEGAMA

CUPHIC

FRIDAT

GURMOE

SNOOPI

Careful!

WHAT YOU MIGHT
END UP WITH IF
YOU HAPPEN TO
TOUCH POISON IVY
WHILE PICKING A
FOUR-LEAF CLOVER.

Now arrange the circled letters
to form the surprise answer, as
suggested by the above cartoon.

Print
answer
here

A " ☐☐☐☐ " OF ☐☐☐☐☐ ☐☐☐☐☐

JUMBLE®

Unscramble these six Jumbles, one letter to each square, to form six ordinary words.

TEAGEN

YEMILT

TINADY

LOOTIN

NISSIT

POWALL

WHAT AN ATTRACTIVE SWEATER SOME—TIMES PULLS.

Now arrange the circled letters to form the surprise answer, as suggested by the above cartoon.

Print answer here ◯◯◯' ◯◯◯◯◯ OVER THE ◯◯◯◯

JUMBLE®

Unscramble these six Jumbles, one letter
to each square, to form six ordinary words.

DUPLED

FOYFAP

TUITOW

NENFLE

PLARIL

EXRILI

This will keep us
busy for a month

WHAT THE TREE
TRIMMER EXPERIENCED
AFTER THE STORM.

Now arrange the circled letters
to form the surprise answer, as
suggested by the above cartoon.

**Print
answer
here**

A "⬡⬡⬡⬡⬡⬡⬡⬡" ⬡⬡⬡⬡⬡⬡

JUMBLE®

Unscramble these six Jumbles, one letter
to each square, to form six ordinary words.

THRIME

DUNJOC

MELLUV

HERBTO

GALENT

DOINIE

Sorry, I'll have
to let you go

HOW THE
STRUGGLING BARBER
MADE A PROFIT.

Now arrange the circled letters
to form the surprise answer, as
suggested by the above cartoon.

*Print
answer
here* HE ☐☐☐ ☐☐☐☐☐☐☐☐

JUMBLE®

Unscramble these six Jumbles, one letter to each square, to form six ordinary words.

DILANI

VENCOL

SHARTH

MAHNLY

MANIAE

CALDIP

WHAT THE ESKIMO SAID TO HIS FRIEND.

Now arrange the circled letters to form the surprise answer, as suggested by the above cartoon.

Print answer here

JUMBLE®

Unscramble these six Jumbles, one letter to each square, to form six ordinary words.

RALYHD

NEDPAX

NEDHIB

TURIVE

TIVLYE

CRADIN

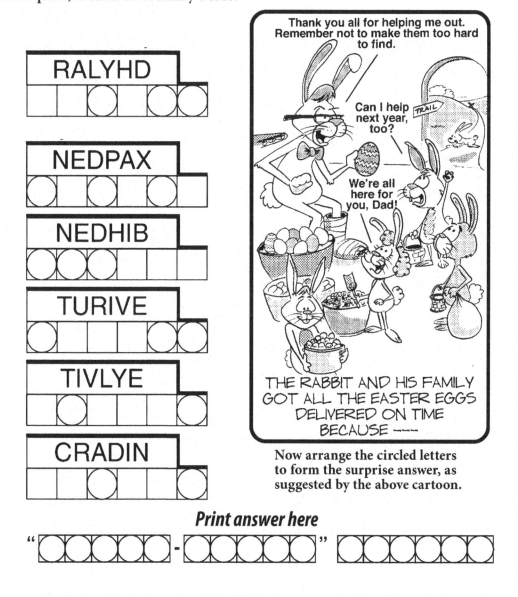

Thank you all for helping me out. Remember not to make them too hard to find.

Can I help next year, too?

TRAIL

We're all here for you, Dad!

THE RABBIT AND HIS FAMILY GOT ALL THE EASTER EGGS DELIVERED ON TIME BECAUSE ----

Now arrange the circled letters to form the surprise answer, as suggested by the above cartoon.

Print answer here

" ◯◯◯◯◯ - ◯◯◯◯◯ " ◯◯◯◯◯

JUMBLE®

Unscramble these six Jumbles, one letter
to each square, to form six ordinary words.

WEKIDC

RIDHEN

MOULEV

CRUPES

HICSWT

CLOTKE

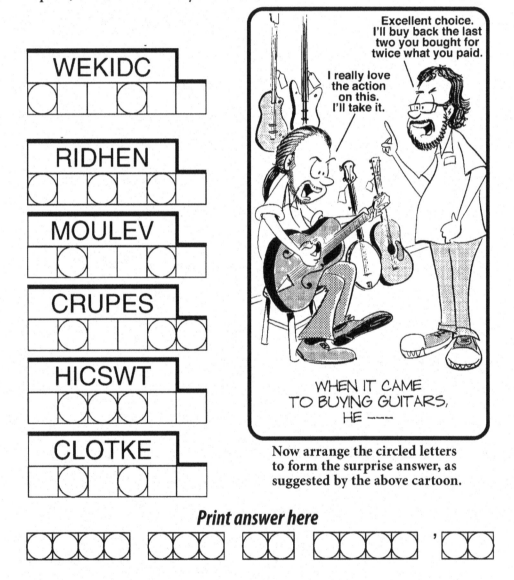

Excellent choice.
I'll buy back the last
two you bought for
twice what you paid.

I really love
the action
on this.
I'll take it.

WHEN IT CAME
TO BUYING GUITARS,
HE ----

Now arrange the circled letters
to form the surprise answer, as
suggested by the above cartoon.

Print answer here

⬡⬡⬡⬡ ⬡⬡⬡ ⬡⬡ ⬡⬡⬡⬡ '⬡⬡

JUMBLE®

Unscramble these six Jumbles, one letter to each square, to form six ordinary words.

WDORAC

PLUCEO

CIVENO

TAYRIF

SAWLEE

KYRNAC

This has always been my students' favorite experiment.

You really know what you're doing.

My sister loved this experiment when she had your class.

Cool!

WHEN IT CAME TO TEACHING CHEMISTRY, THE PROFESSOR HAD IT ---

Now arrange the circled letters to form the surprise answer, as suggested by the above cartoon.

Print answer here

JUMBLE®

Unscramble these six Jumbles, one letter
to each square, to form six ordinary words.

CIYIOD

MBENUR

MICONE

NARPIS

SSALPH

NLUUGP

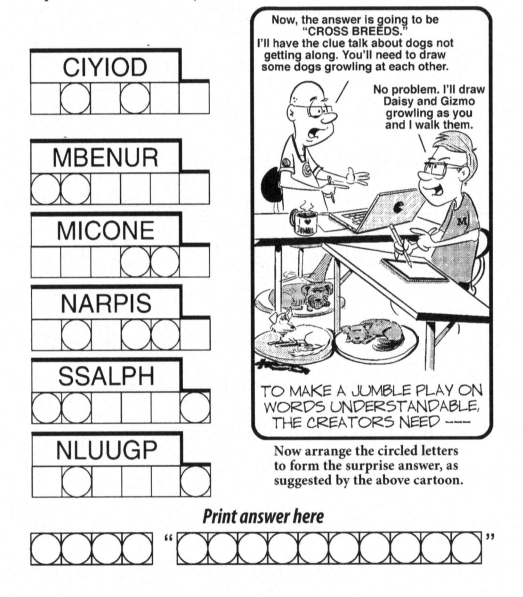

Now, the answer is going to be
"CROSS BREEDS."
I'll have the clue talk about dogs not
getting along. You'll need to draw
some dogs growling at each other.

No problem. I'll draw
Daisy and Gizmo
growling as you
and I walk them.

TO MAKE A JUMBLE PLAY ON
WORDS UNDERSTANDABLE,
THE CREATORS NEED ----

Now arrange the circled letters
to form the surprise answer, as
suggested by the above cartoon.

Print answer here

" "

JUMBLE®

Unscramble these six Jumbles, one letter
to each square, to form six ordinary words.

MRHHYT

RUUENS

SELOCT

SOCIAM

RANBER

SNEAKH

People love
our brittle.
What are our
earnings this
quarter?

Let me
total our
sales.

I love
fresh
brittle.

TO FIND OUT HOW MUCH
MONEY THE NEW PEANUT
BRITTLE COMPANY WAS
MAKING, THEY NEEDED TO ----

Now arrange the circled letters
to form the surprise answer, as
suggested by the above cartoon.

Print answer here

JUMBLE®

Unscramble these six Jumbles, one letter to each square, to form six ordinary words.

CAFTEF

VATENI

YENANO

EGGANE

SINIHF

GAUTOE

Why do you always have to shine brighter than me?

What are you talking about? I thought we were friends.

I can control the lights by remote.

That's great.

THE LIGHT BULBS DIDN'T ALWAYS GET ALONG. THEIR RELATIONSHIP WAS ---

Now arrange the circled letters to form the surprise answer, as suggested by the above cartoon.

Print answer here

◯◯-◯◯◯◯◯, ◯◯◯-◯◯◯◯◯

JUMBLE®

Unscramble these six Jumbles, one letter to each square, to form six ordinary words.

WSLAAY

NEGLET

LULHIP

MIOCEN

FIREVY

KEDDDI

On the sunny side, the temperature can reach 123 Celsius. On the dark side, it can be minus 153 Celsius.

How can it be so different?

THE DIFFERENCE BETWEEN THE DARK SIDE OF THE MOON AND THE LIGHT SIDE IS ---

Now arrange the circled letters to form the surprise answer, as suggested by the above cartoon.

Print answer here

Answers

1. **Jumbles:** MOUTH FEVER PSYCHE UPLIFT
   Answer: What the taxidermist's personality certainly was—
   "STUFFY"

2. **Jumbles:** OBESE BALMY HAMMER THEORY
   Answer: People with wanderlust seldom feel this—
   AT HOME AT HOME

3. **Jumbles:** GUESS AFTER KIDNAP ROBBER
   Answer: The longer that sergeant stayed in the army—
   THE "RANKER" HE GOT

4. **Jumbles:** GLORY LINER DABBLE FORGET
   Answer: What her attempts at cooking brought him—TO A BOIL

5. **Jumbles:** DELVE CARGO BUCKET LAYMAN
   Answer: What was Michaelangelo's favorite dessert?—
   MARBLE CAKE

6. **Jumbles:** FOYER PANDA BUSILY GAMBLE
   Answer: How the sponge divers found their work—
   "ABSORBING"

7. **Jumbles:** PIKER ABBOT HOMAGE CLERGY
   Answer: What lightning gave the Frankenstein monster—
   A BIG "CHARGE"

8. **Jumbles:** SNOWY CATCH INLAID GYRATE
   Answer: How the miser got rich—THE "HOARD" WAY

9. **Jumbles:** THINK VIXEN MYSELF SAFARI
   Answer: What the fisherman's gross income was—
   SAME AS HIS "NET"

10. **Jumbles:** AISLE COACH FORGER DURESS
    Answer: What that math whiz who rose to the top of the firm
    ended up as—THE FIGURE HEAD

11. **Jumbles:** HANDY AMUSE YELLOW DISCUS
    Answer: What the highway maintenance man was told to do—
    MEND HIS "WAY"

12. **Jumbles:** FLAKE BLOOM FUTURE TONGUE
    Answer: How to silence a "loud" tie—GET A "MUFFLER"

13. **Jumbles:** HURRY BISON GRATIS FORKED
    Answer: What the professional crap shooter's business must
    have been—"SHAKY"

14. **Jumbles:** LEGAL MOOSE RAREFY HICCUP
    Answer: Praise this and you're sure to turn a woman's head—
    HER PROFILE

15. **Jumbles:** LOONY FOUNT ORPHAN GUITAR
    Answer: Why they found the nudist camp so boring—
    NOTHING WENT ON

16. **Jumbles:** HOARD SKULL UPTOWN FLORID
    Answer: How the manicurist rejected his proposal of
    marriage—OUT OF HAND

17. **Jumbles:** FINAL DERBY NUANCE HOURLY
    Answer: Another name for a dialogue—A DOUBLE "CHIN"

18. **Jumbles:** AGENT EIGHT GENTRY MORBID
    Answer: She was always sure to keep a secret—GOING

19. **Jumbles:** AHEAD CABIN FIASCO IMPEND
    Answer: Apparently it's a sign of good manners to put up with
    this—BAD ONES

20. **Jumbles:** ODIUM WHOOP AGENCY CAMPER
    Answer: What the first day of the week can be—"MOAN" DAY

21. **Jumbles:** GOOSE ANKLE PARITY SAVAGE
    Answer: What their babies' bedroom was called—THE "NOISERY"

22. **Jumbles:** LINGO BOGUS GOLFER DRAGON
    Answer: What they said when they saw the Grand Canyon—
    "GORGES"

23. **Jumbles:** LUSTY AGONY GYPSUM PRAYER
    Answer: Keeping up with the Joneses might also involve
    keeping up with these—THE PAYMENTS

24. **Jumbles:** BROOK GROOM SUNDAE CIPHER
    Answer: What those society "crumbs" were held together
    by—"DOUGH"

25. **Jumbles:** SHINY EJECT RUBBER MIDDAY
    Answer: What the billionaire left when he died—
    MUCH TO BE DESIRED

26. **Jumbles:** IRONY ADMIT FOMENT DOUBLE
    Answer: Permissive parents don't mind when their kids this—
    DON'T MIND

27. **Jumbles:** COCOA OUTDO BUTTER ZENITH
    Answer: He doesn't like to be ordered around unless it's this—
    A ROUND OF BOOZE

28. **Jumbles:** RIGOR GAMUT SOLACE RATION
    Answer: What she wished her admirers would practice—
    "ARMS" CONTROL

29. **Jumbles:** GRIMY ERUPT FEUDAL JESTER
    Answer: What an unethical trustee sometimes ends up as—
    A TRUSTY

30. **Jumbles:** AWFUL PAPER JETSAM HINDER
    Answer: What nepotism means in the field of employment—
    TO PUT ON "HEIRS"

31. **Jumbles:** MURKY WHILE JACKAL RAMROD
    Answer: A four-letter word that some people find most
    "objectionable"—WORK

32. **Jumbles:** BLOOD EXACT MARTIN JAGUAR
    Answer: A boxer who fails to carry out his second's suggestions
    is sometimes this—CARRIED OUT

33. **Jumbles:** SIXTY RABBI EASILY NEARLY
    Answer: One is not at liberty to take this with others—LIBERTIES

34. **Jumbles:** NOISY REBEL MARAUD SQUALL
    Answer: What the bodybuilder turned clam digger seemed to
    be—"MUSSEL"-BOUND

35. **Jumbles:** FANCY OFTEN NOZZLE RADIAL
    Answer: What that tiresome speechmaker could not be after he
    was called on—CALLED OFF

36. **Jumbles:** DUCHY USURP BONNET MISUSE
    Answer: His worst fault is telling other people—THEIRS

37. **Jumbles:** AGILE GRAVE BREACH FENNEL
    Answer: What a brand-new father is about to enter into—
    A CHANGING WORLD

38. **Jumbles:** UNCAP TRACT FRIGID IODINE
    Answer: What many people start out on, right after they return
    home from a vacation—AN EGO TRIP

39. **Jumbles:** GLAND FETID NIMBLE DROWSY
    Answer: What a person who's always kicking seldom has—
    A LEG TO STAND ON

40. **Jumbles:** MOGUL JULEP BRIDGE COMMON
    Answer: If a pedestrian is prone to be careless he might end up
    this way—PRONE

41. **Jumbles:** FINIS ALIAS INFANT MISERY
    Answer: What many an amateur gardener gets for his pains—
    LINIMENT

42. **Jumbles:** MANGY SUMAC DOUBLY GATHER
    Answer: A man who is always asking for a loan is apt to be left
    this—ALONE

43. **Jumbles:** NOVEL DRAMA BYGONE SCHEME
    Answer: Credit might be the means to live like this—
    BEYOND ONE'S MEANS

44. **Jumbles:** GRIEF PAUSE EROTIC COLUMN
    Answer: You can't get rid of a bad temper by doing this—
    LOSING IT

45. **Jumbles:** HOUSE CRAWL OCCULT URCHIN
    Answer: Another name for the time you spend going home
    from work—THE "CRUSH" HOUR

46. **Jumbles:** ADULT GLOVE FLABBY LEVITY
Answer: Add this on for your protection, if you're about to invest—"IGATE"

47. **Jumbles:** BASSO WEARY RITUAL MASCOT
Answer: His clothes tell you a lot about this—HIS "WEAR"-ABOUTS

48. **Jumbles:** TRYST DUCAL BRIDLE HANGAR
Answer: He's old enough to know better, but too old to do this—CARE

49. **Jumbles:** TULLE FUDGE PELVIS SUPERB
Answer: What a good insecticide might be —A "PEST" SELLER

50. **Jumbles:** SOGGY FRANC INCOME ATOMIC
Answer: It's hard to raise a child, especially when it's this—MORNING

51. **Jumbles:** STYLE FENCE SPRAIN TRUSTY
Answer: The campers are receiving their gifts right now…They are getting—PRESENT "TENTS"

52. **Jumbles:** ELOPE UNIFY CUSTOM AFRAID
Answer: After losing his lease, the owner of the plant nursery would be—UPROOTED

53. **Jumbles:** ODDLY MUNCH UNFAIR HOLLOW
Answer: Cities might one day be built on the lunar surface, which could result in a—FULL MOON

54. **Jumbles:** WAIVE SPOIL AVENUE SPRAWL
Answer: The new quarterback didn't get excited about much. The coach worried that he was too—PASSIVE

55. **Jumbles:** ADMIT YEAST OUTLET MAGNET
Answer: He wanted to start an apple orchard, but to get it going, he needed—SEED MONEY

56. **Jumbles:** WACKY SPURN LATELY EMERGE
Answer: The janitors' softball team's tournament victory was a—CLEAN SWEEP

57. **Jumbles:** GAVEL GRIND DISMAL ARTERY
Answer: Conditions at the school were—DEGRADING

58. **Jumbles:** GLORY HEFTY INFUSE GOVERN
Answer: During the ghosts' football game, the band played their—"FRIGHT" SONG

59. **Jumbles:** SHINY GOING WISDOM INFANT
Answer: She had to give up tennis for a while, but she was now back in the—SWING OF THINGS

60. **Jumbles:** GOURD AFTER ORNERY BOUNCE
Answer: The carpenter was done with the new door. He exited after making a—GOOD ENTRANCE

61. **Jumbles:** AVOID CHAOS FINALE CHERUB
Answer: The postage stamps featuring the Mt. Rushmore carvings sold for—FACE VALUE

62. **Jumbles:** OFTEN EAGLE HICCUP TRAUMA
Answer: He wanted to change the channel, but he didn't have a—REMOTE CHANCE

63. **Jumbles:** WHEAT EVOKE REGRET TYCOON
Answer: The more tournaments the tennis player won, the more he was able to enjoy his—NET WORTH

64. **Jumbles:** HOUSE UPEND IMPISH BICKER
Answer: Even though the Scarecrow didn't have a brain, he—SPOKE HIS MIND

65. **Jumbles:** BOGUS FAULT APIECE GLANCE
Answer: He stole second and now led the league in steals which pleased his—FANBASE

66. **Jumbles:** ORBIT SHOVE DEPUTY MASCOT
Answer: After constant complaints about his salad, the customer was going to get—TOSSED OUT

67. **Jumbles:** DERBY ELECT MORTAL BANTER
Answer: When Sherlock Holmes was in grammar school, solving a mystery was—ELEMENTARY

68. **Jumbles:** PIANO TOKEN PEOPLE FRUGAL
Answer: The hospital's new surgery center was in—FULL OPERATION

69. **Jumbles:** VOWEL EMCEE SHIFTY DOLLAR
Answer: The retired tennis star displayed the tennis racquet that had—SERVED HIM WELL

70. **Jumbles:** DOILY AWARD JOVIAL GOATEE
Answer: She'd hiked to the top of this mountain before. She really liked the—DEJA "VIEW"

71. **Jumbles:** PRIOR GUESS BEFALL KITTEN
Answer: The soccer team's goalie was amazing. He was a—KEEPER

72. **Jumbles:** STUNG BRINK SICKEN EXOTIC
Answer: The fight between the elephants featured—BOXING TRUNKS

73. **Jumbles:** ANKLE GUARD THRIVE WALLOP
Answer: When the sisters started a business together, they were—WORK-RELATED

74. **Jumbles:** AMUSE ELECT DIVINE EFFORT
Answer: When the clocks came to life, they were able to get some—FACE TIME

75. **Jumbles:** SCOFF ONION MULLET EIGHTY
Answer: The dogs thought that digging up the yard was a—"HOLE" LOT OF FUN

76. **Jumbles:** OOMPH TRUTH MISUSE FINALE
Answer: The Jumble creators usually call it a day when they—"PUN" OUT OF STEAM

77. **Jumbles:** AWARE HOUSE MISFIT MODEST
Answer: The most commonly spoken language in the bakery was—"SWEETISH"

78. **Jumbles:** PRIOR SNIFF ADMIRE GENDER
Answer: When the zombie twins played horseshoes, they were—DEAD RINGERS

79. **Jumbles:** ABOUT ENACT ENROLL VERMIN
Answer: After adding central air conditioning, they experienced—"VENT-ELATION"

80. **Jumbles:** STASH CYNIC PRIMER ZENITH
Answer: Ellis Island was the gateway for millions of immigrants who arrived on—CITIZEN SHIPS

81. **Jumbles:** CELLO PRUNE MASCOT PUNDIT
Answer: The money she earned selling vitamins and other nutrients was —SUPPLEMENTAL

82. **Jumbles:** HUMID LARVA BAFFLE LOTION
Answer: The crowded church service was—"FAITH-FULL"

83. **Jumbles:** PRIOR WHILE GRAVEL PONCHO
Answer: Electricity in Heaven is provided by a—HIGHER POWER

84. **Jumbles:** CRAMP DICEY UNWIND LEGEND
Answer: The author hoped her latest diet book would appeal to a—WIDER AUDIENCE

85. **Jumbles:** POISE DOUGH PAYDAY POLICE
Answer: He thought that having life insurance was a—GOOD POLICY

86. **Jumbles:** EXERT TAKEN OSPREY TROWEL
Answer: The collector of classic films owned—"REEL" ESTATE

87. **Jumbles:** PIVOT PRIMP DEFUSE WEALTH
Answer: When they printed the carton upside down on April Fool's Day, some people—FLIPPED

88. **Jumbles:** HEDGE RISKY FINALE UNWISE
Answer: He planned to wash and wax his car early today and was ready to—RISE AND SHINE

89. **Jumbles:** MURKY DRESS LAWMAN UTOPIA
Answer: After he stole the ball, making the basket was going to be a—SLAM DUNK

90. **Jumbles:** DOUSE BROKE DAMAGE BEFORE
Answer: Al Capone's favorite restaurant was usually—MOBBED

91. **Jumbles:** EXPEL DRIFT DECEIT MUZZLE
Answer: His high credit card bill was a—"DUE-ZIE"

92. **Jumbles:** PETTY EVOKE CUSTOM DAINTY
Answer: After being so rude to the doctor, he was about to become an—OUT-PATIENT

93. **Jumbles:** OZONE SKIMP SHREWD GOALIE
Answer: With so many children trying out the equipment, the new playground had—MOOD SWINGS

94. **Jumbles:** SKIER GLOAT WINERY DECENT
Answer: The four-star general opened his own restaurant and loved—TAKING ORDERS

95. **Jumbles:** TREND ROBOT LOCALE LIKELY
Answer: The calico didn't get along with the cat that was—KITTY-CORNER

96. **Jumbles:** GOUGE DRANK SHOULD PIRACY
Answer: The guitarist's favorite pants were—"CHORD-UROYS"

97. **Jumbles:** EMCEE DODGE ABACUS BODILY
Answer: The beavers' home had been there for years, but now it was—DAM-AGED

98. **Jumbles:** HENCE MOGUL ODDEST PARDON
Answer: The male college cheerleaders' favorite meal consisted of—"RAH-MEN" NOODLES

99. **Jumbles:** BRIBE MINCE HECTIC PURSER
Answer: Two, three, five, and seven will always be—IN THEIR PRIME

100. **Jumbles:** EPOXY MADLY OUTAGE PANTRY
Answer: To start his new job at the nuclear power plant, he needed to—GET UP AND "ATOM"

101. **Jumbles:** BRAWL GLAND APIECE OBLIGE
Answer: The crane loved her new phone and really enjoyed the—CALL "WADING"

102. **Jumbles:** RATIO DIGIT APATHY INFUSE
Answer: They thought their new garbage can was animal-proof, but the animals—TRASHED IT

103. **Jumbles:** QUAKE PUTTY INSIST PURSUE
Answer: Her mom's sister had a lot of old furniture, which she considered—"AUNT-IQUES"

104. **Jumbles:** METAL MOUTH RABBIT ISLAND
Answer: The hen couldn't find her eggs after she—MISLAID THEM

105. **Jumbles:** MERGE VALET DROWSY HYPHEN
Answer: Her husband had made plans to build her a new bookcase today, but he—SHELVED THEM

106. **Jumbles:** FACET APART INFAMY MODULE
Answer: Not charging as much on their credit cards—PAID OFF

107. **Jumbles:** STOMP PROOF ICONIC ANNUAL
Answer: The math teacher was being reprimanded because of his—INFRACTIONS

108. **Jumbles:** BOSSY EXILE UNTOLD SHREWD
Answer: The golf course was for sale. The owner wanted to sell the—"HOLE" BUSINESS

109. **Jumbles:** GUESS MONEY SLOWLY INLAND
Answer: Owning a dictionary without pages is—MEANINGLESS

110. **Jumbles:** ARROW LOFTY LONGER PALLET
Answer: Sick in bed, Mom wouldn't let him go to practice until he could—PLAY WELL

111. **Jumbles:** WINDY KOALA MODEST ARTERY
Answer: Mother Nature was often busy on clear, damp mornings, because she had—LOTS TO "DEW"

112. **Jumbles:** ADDED WINCE HIDDEN IMMUNE
Answer: When the kids complained at dinner, their parents were being—"WHINED" AND DINED

113. **Jumbles:** WOUND BURLY GOVERN LOOSEN
Answer: After rolling 12 strikes in a row for a 300, he was—BOWLED OVER

114. **Jumbles:** WAFER HOIST WIGGLE THORNY
Answer: He didn't want to go tubing, but he did to—GO WITH THE FLOW

115. **Jumbles:** SHAKY FRONT MADDER ENCORE
Answer: Doctors at veterans' hospital dedicate their lives to treating the—"HARMED" FORCES

116. **Jumbles:** BRIAR LOUSY DOCKET CLOUDY
Answer: The Rolling Stones have been together so long, because, as a group, they are—ROCK SOLID

117. **Jumbles:** FUDGE HOBBY BOTTOM ADMIRE
Answer: The cow was late for the big get-together because she hadn't—"HERD" ABOUT IT

118. **Jumbles:** NEWLY WIDTH ENGULF IMPORT
Answer: He took the double. Maybe he could have tripled, but he didn't want to—FIND OUT

119. **Jumbles:** DIRTY HONEY PAYDAY DILUTE
Answer: Tom Cruise played a pilot in "Top Gun" after he—LANDED THE PART

120. **Jumbles:** VINYL BATTY EXODUS ACTUAL
Answer: When asked if he liked the new four-stringed instrument, he said this—"ABSO-LUTE-LY'

121. **Jumbles:** BEACH PATIO GAMBLE BECAME
Answer: The contractor wanted to build more houses, so he built a—HOME PAGE

122. **Jumbles:** PITCH VAGUE RADIUS INDUCT
Answer: When the baker made a wedding cake for his daughter, he was—"TIERING" UP

123. **Jumbles:** GLAZE ISSUE EQUITY FLAVOR
Answer: The priest took his workout routine very seriously and went to the gym—RELIGIOUSLY

124. **Jumbles:** PUSHY FRAUD ORNERY EXOTIC
Answer: All the students who graduated from skydiving school were—DROP-OUTS

125. **Jumbles:** ITCHY SWOON EYELID ATTEND
Answer: Sleepy Hollow's horseman maintained his speed in spite of the—HEADWINDS

126. **Jumbles:** NUTTY FUNKY PARADE EXPERT
Answer: The rare Lincoln one-cent coin cost a—PRETTY PENNY

127. **Jumbles:** ONION KAYAK MEADOW CASHEW
Answer: After going fishing for the first time, he was—HOOKED

128. **Jumbles:** VOUCH FOYER NEATLY FINITE
Answer: She asked her sister if she could borrow a dress, but her sister wasn't—IN FAVOR OF IT

129. **Jumbles:** WHEEL LOGIC ASYLUM INFLUX
Answer: The hospital patients weren't getting along because of all the—ILL WILL

130. **Jumbles:** ABIDE GUMBO CAREER ASTRAY
Answer: How widespread would the fog be tomorrow morning? It was a bit of a—GRAY AREA

131. **Jumbles:** MERCY VENUE INFANT DELUGE
Answer: The casino put in new slots to attract customers and was able to—REEL 'EM IN

132. **Jumbles:** RUGBY DOUSE OPENLY DEFECT
Answer: The Jumble author's new apprentice was happy to be the —"UNDERSTUDY"

133. **Jumbles:** GUEST EQUAL FROSTY TAUGHT
Answer: The boxer who became a baseball player was a—SLUGGER

134. **Jumbles:** TEMPT QUOTA IRONIC VACUUM
Answer: He complained about his job incessantly. His wife told him to—QUIT IT

135. **Jumbles:** VALID CLASH DRAGON POCKET
Answer: The speedy barber was moving—AT A GOOD CLIP

136. **Jumbles:** ABACK BRAND KETTLE JOVIAL
Answer: The bunny had a problem changing the flat. Thankfully, he could call a—JACK-RABBIT

137. **Jumbles:** VITAL RAYON WOBBLE DREDGE
Answer: When it came to the design of his new yacht, he—WENT OVERBOARD

138. **Jumbles:** FLEET BAULT FIASCO TROPHY
Answer: To make the triple play, the defense needed an—ALL-OUT EFFORT

139. **Jumbles:** SNIFF IRONY KERNEL INNING
Answer: The two plumbers installing the bathroom fixtures were working—"IN-SINK"

140. **Jumbles:** ADAGE JUDGE KITTEN HYPHEN
Answer: The pilot's three-line poem spoken at 30,000 feet was a—'HIGH-KU'

141. **Jumbles:** WHILE BLURB HEARTH ADRIFT
Answer: The bridge pair argued constantly, so their opponents hoped they'd—BID FAREWELL

142. **Jumbles:** FLUTE LLAMA SHROUD TARIFF
Answer: The chef who wouldn't try food prepared by other chefs was—FULL OF HIMSELF

143. **Jumbles:** MODEM LINER SMOOTH QUARRY
Answer: The poet just quit. She stopped writing poetry. There was no—RHYME OR REASON

144. **Jumbles:** BOOTH KNELT DRESSY PAYOUT
Answer: The computer whiz loved his new electronic piano. He was a natural—ON THE KEYBOARD

145. **Jumbles:** NEEDY SLUSH DROWSY CANVAS
Answer: The tennis players stopped playing when—LUNCH WAS SERVED

146. **Jumbles:** SHRUG DAISY FORGOT ACTIVE
Answer: The cemetery's new security guard worked the—GRAVEYARD SHIFT

147. **Jumbles:** AVOID GROWL FILLET BOVINE
Answer: With winter over, spring was this to the trees—A "RE-LEAF"

148. **Jumbles:** CROWN TOPAZ EXCEED SKIMPY
Answer: They worked on the song separately, and then—COMPARED NOTES

149. **Jumbles:** MOUND SHOWN STIGMA CANOPY
Answer: The last time humans walked on the lunar surface, it was—MANY MOONS AGO

150. **Jumbles:** GRUNT MESSY TRICKY IMPEDED
Answer: When children played with their new Slinky toys in April of 1946, it was—SPRINGTIME

151. **Jumbles:** NOVEL PLUME SNEEZE FORMAT
Answer: The elegant new box seats at the baseball stadium were—"FAN-SEE"

152. **Jumbles:** ELOPE BRICK RATHER PODIUM
Answer: The chemists ate lunch every day at the—PERIODIC TABLE

153. **Jumbles:** SHINY CLOCK MAGNET SQUARE
Answer: The fishermen wanted to reel in some fish, but they were only able to— CATCH SOME RAYS

154. **Jumbles:** GLOAT IMPEL SUDDEN ABSURD
Answer: When they figured out how to write down music, it was—NOTABLE

155. **Jumbles:** FEWER THIRD MOTIVE JOGGER
Answer: The first traffic light ever installed was popular—FROM THE GET-GO

156. **Jumbles:** CARRY TABOO UNLIKE WARMTH
Answer: Henry David proofread "Walden" carefully. After all, he was known for his—"THOREAU" WORK

157. **Jumbles:** ALLOW HALVE TURKEY DRAFTY
Answer: For the purse-snatcher, getting caught was—HARD TO TAKE

158. **Jumbles:** HONEY ORBIT WEAKEN CAVIAR
Answer: After watching their team blow a huge lead, the beer pub turned into a—"WHINE" BAR

159. **Jumbles:** EXERT HAVEN TROPHY SYMBOL
Answer: Their business was on a street with many shops and another one was opening—NEXT "STORE"

160. **Jumbles:** NEWLY GRUFF BEYOND BLAZER
Answer: The new employee at the nuclear power plant was a—BUNDLE OF ENERGY

161. **Jumbles:** FUTILE UPLIFT PRIMER DEVICE THWART DOMINO
Answer: Why Atlas was arrested—HE HELD UP THE WORLD

162. **Jumbles:** TRYING ALBINO SUBURB BELFRY MALLET DECEIT
Answer: A man who likes you to be at his service—THE MINISTER

163. **Jumbles:** FILLET GUZZLE KISMET JIGGLE INLAND BANNER
Answer: What the captain had when he saw the iceberg—A SINKING FEELING

164. **Jumbles:** PARADE COLUMN GAMBIT BOUYED LADING THRASH
Answer: How he returned home from a vacation at a gambling resort—POUNDS LIGHTER

165. **Jumbles:** BANISH MASCOT DEADLY ASSURE IGUANA GIBLET
Answer: What they said about the psychiatrist—MIND'S HIS BUSINESS

166. **Jumbles:** NEARBY ADMIRE MUFFLE PARODY INTACT HAMMER
Answer: What you might eat at a buffet dinner—A "BALANCED" DIET

167. **Jumbles:** PALATE HARDLY NEARLY CANOPY ENZYME QUIVER
Answer: What applause usually is—THE "ZEAL" OF APPROVAL

168. **Jumbles:** EYEFUL BUCKET EXOTIC QUAINT MINGLE CENSUS
Answer: What a big noise at the office often is at home—A LITTLE SQUEAK

169. **Jumbles:** TINKLE DAMAGE HICCUP ADRIFT MORGUE POISON
Answer: What you might end up with if you happen to touch poison ivy while picking a four-leaf clover—A "RASH" OF GOOD LUCK

170. **Jumbles:** NEGATE TIMELY DAINTY LOTION INSIST WALLOP
Answer: What an attractive sweater sometimes pulls—MEN'S EYES OVER THE WOOL

171. **Jumbles:** PUDDLE PAYOFF OUTWIT FENNEL PILLAR ELIXIR
Answer: What the tree trimmer experienced after the storm—A "WINDFALL" PROFIT

172. **Jumbles:** HERMIT JOCUND VELLUM BROTHER TANGLE IODINE
Answer: How the struggling barber made a profit—HE CUT OVERHEAD

173. **Jumbles:** INLAID CLOVEN THRASH HYMNAL ANEMIA PLACID
Answer: What the eskimo said to his friend—HAVE AN ICE DAY

174. **Jumbles:** HARDLY EXPAND BEHIND VIRTUE LEVITY RANCID
Answer: The rabbit and his family got all the Easter eggs delivered on time because—"EVERY-BUNNY" HELPED

175. **Jumbles:** WICKED HINDER VOLUME SPRUCE SWITCH LOCKET
Answer: When it came to buying guitars he—KNEW HOW TO PICK 'EM

176. **Jumbles:** COWARD COUPLE NOVICE RATIFY WEASEL CRANKY
Answer: When it came to teaching chemistry, the professor had it—DOWN TO A SCIENCE

177. **Jumbles:** IDIOCY NUMBER INCOME SPRAIN SPLASH UNPLUG
Answer: To make a Jumble play on words understandable, the creators need—GOOD "PUNMANSHIP"

178. **Jumbles:** RHYTHM UNSURE CLOSET MOSAIC BARREN SHAKEN
Answer: To find out how much money the new peanut brittle company was making, they needed to—CRUNCH SOME NUMBERS

179. **Jumbles:** AFFECT NATIVE ANYONE ENGAGE FINISH OUTAGE
Answer: The light bulbs didn't always get along. Their relationship was—ON-AGAIN, OFF-AGAIN

180. **Jumbles:** ALWAYS GENTLE UPHILL INCOME VERIFY KIDDED
Answer: The difference between the dark side of the moon and the light side is—LIKE NIGHT AND DAY

Need More Jumbles?

Order any of these books through your bookseller or call Triumph Books toll-free at 800-335-5323.

Jumble® Books

More than 175 puzzles each!

Cowboy Jumble®
ISBN: 978-1-62937-355-3

Jammin' Jumble®
ISBN: 1-57243-844-4

Java Jumble®
ISBN: 978-1-60078-415-6

Jazzy Jumble®
ISBN: 978-1-57243-962-7

Jet Set Jumble®
ISBN: 978-1-60078-353-1

Joyful Jumble®
ISBN: 978-1-60078-079-0

Juke Joint Jumble®
ISBN: 978-1-60078-295-4

Jumble® Anniversary
ISBN: 987-1-62937-734-6

Jumble® at Work
ISBN: 1-57243-147-4

Jumble® Ballet
ISBN: 978-1-62937-616-5

Jumble® Birthday
ISBN: 978-1-62937-652-3

Jumble® Celebration
ISBN: 978-1-60078-134-6

Jumble® Circus
ISBN: 978-1-60078-739-3

Jumble® Cuisine
ISBN: 978-1-62937-735-3

Jumble® Drag Race
ISBN: 978-1-62937-483-3

Jumble® Ever After
ISBN: 978-1-62937-785-8

Jumble® Explorer
ISBN: 978-1-60078-854-3

Jumble® Explosion
ISBN: 978-1-60078-078-3

Jumble® Fever
ISBN: 1-57243-593-3

Jumble® Fiesta
ISBN: 1-57243-626-3

Jumble® Fun
ISBN: 1-57243-379-5

Jumble® Galaxy
ISBN: 978-1-60078-583-2

Jumble® Garden
ISBN: 978-1-62937-653-0

Jumble® Genius
ISBN: 1-57243-896-7

Jumble® Geography
ISBN: 978-1-62937-615-8

Jumble® Getaway
ISBN: 978-1-60078-547-4

Jumble® Gold
ISBN: 978-1-62937-354-6

Jumble® Grab Bag
ISBN: 1-57243-273-X

Jumble® Gymnastics
ISBN: 978-1-62937-306-5

Jumble® Jackpot
ISBN: 1-57243-897-5

Jumble® Jailbreak
ISBN: 978-1-62937-002-6

Jumble® Jambalaya
ISBN: 978-1-60078-294-7

Jumble® Jamboree
ISBN: 1-57243-696-4

Jumble® Jitterbug
ISBN: 978-1-60078-584-9

Jumble® Journey
ISBN: 978-1-62937-549-6

Jumble® Jubilation
ISBN: 978-1-62937-784-1

Jumble® Jubilee
ISBN: 1-57243-231-4

Jumble® Juggernaut
ISBN: 978-1-60078-026-4

Jumble® Junction
ISBN: 1-57243-380-9

Jumble® Jungle
ISBN: 978-1-57243-961-0

Jumble® Kingdom
ISBN: 978-1-62937-079-8

Jumble® Knockout
ISBN: 978-1-62937-078-1

Jumble® Madness
ISBN: 1-892049-24-4

Jumble® Magic
ISBN: 978-1-60078-795-9

Jumble® Marathon
ISBN: 978-1-60078-944-1

Jumble® Neighbor
ISBN: 978-1-62937-845-9

Jumble® Parachute
ISBN: 978-1-62937-548-9

Jumble® Safari
ISBN: 978-1-60078-675-4

Jumble® See & Search
ISBN: 1-57243-549-6

Jumble® See & Search 2
ISBN: 1-57243-734-0

Jumble® Sensation
ISBN: 978-1-60078-548-1

Jumble® Surprise
ISBN: 1-57243-320-5

Jumble® Symphony
ISBN: 978-1-62937-131-3

Jumble® Theater
ISBN: 978-1-62937-484-03

Jumble® University
ISBN: 978-1-62937-001-9

Jumble® Unleashed
ISBN: 978-1-62937-844-2

Jumble® Vacation
ISBN: 978-1-60078-796-6

Jumble® Wedding
ISBN: 978-1-62937-307-2

Jumble® Workout
ISBN: 978-1-60078-943-4

Jumpin' Jumble®
ISBN: 978-1-60078-027-1

Lunar Jumble®
ISBN: 978-1-60078-853-6

Monster Jumble®
ISBN: 978-1-62937-213-6

Mystic Jumble®
ISBN: 978-1-62937-130-6

Outer Space Jumble®
ISBN: 978-1-60078-416-3

Rainy Day Jumble®
ISBN: 978-1-60078-352-4

Ready, Set, Jumble®
ISBN: 978-1-60078-133-0

Rock 'n' Roll Jumble®
ISBN: 978-1-60078-674-7

Royal Jumble®
ISBN: 978-1-60078-738-6

Sports Jumble®
ISBN: 1-57243-113-X

Summer Fun Jumble®
ISBN: 1-57243-114-8

Touchdown Jumble®
ISBN: 978-1-62937-212-9

Travel Jumble®
ISBN: 1-57243-198-9

TV Jumble®
ISBN: 1-57243-461-9

Oversize Jumble® Books

More than 500 puzzles each!

Generous Jumble®
ISBN: 1-57243-385-X

Giant Jumble®
ISBN: 1-57243-349-3

Gigantic Jumble®
ISBN: 1-57243-426-0

Jumbo Jumble®
ISBN: 1-57243-314-0

The Very Best of Jumble® BrainBusters
ISBN: 1-57243-845-2

Jumble® Crosswords™

More than 175 puzzles each!

More Jumble® Crosswords™
ISBN: 1-57243-386-8

Jumble® Crosswords™ Jackpot
ISBN: 1-57243-615-8

Jumble® Crosswords™ Jamboree
ISBN: 1-57243-787-1

Jumble® BrainBusters™

More than 175 puzzles each!

Jumble® BrainBusters™
ISBN: 1-892049-28-7

Jumble® BrainBusters™ II
ISBN: 1-57243-424-4

Jumble® BrainBusters™ III
ISBN: 1-57243-463-5

Jumble® BrainBusters™ IV
ISBN: 1-57243-489-9

Jumble® BrainBusters™ 5
ISBN: 1-57243-548-8

Jumble® BrainBusters™ Bonanza
ISBN: 1-57243-616-6

Boggle™ BrainBusters™
ISBN: 1-57243-592-5

Boggle™ BrainBusters™ 2
ISBN: 1-57243-788-X

Jumble® BrainBusters™ Junior
ISBN: 1-892049-29-5

Jumble® BrainBusters™ Junior II
ISBN: 1-57243-425-2

Fun in the Sun with Jumble® BrainBusters™
ISBN: 1-57243-733-2